Leveraging Chaos

The Mysteries of Leadership and Policy Revealed

John R. Shoup and Susan Clark Studer

Rowman & Littlefield Education
A division of
Rowman & Littlefield Publishers, Inc.
Lanham • New York • Toronto • Plymouth, UK

Published by Rowman & Littlefield Education
A division of Rowman & Littlefield Publishers, Inc.
A wholly owned subsidary of The Rowman & Littlefield Publishing Group, Inc.
4501 Forbes Boulevard, Suite 200, Lanham, Maryland 20706
http://www.rowmaneducation.com

Estover Road, Plymouth PL6 7PY, United Kingdom

British Library Cataloguing in Publication Information Available

Library of Congress Cataloging-in-Publication Data
Shoup, John R.
    Leveraging chaos : the mysteries of leadership and policy revealed / John R. Shoup and Susan Clark Studer.
        p.   cm.
    Includes bibliographical references and index.
    ISBN 978-1-60709-756-3 (cloth : alk. paper) — ISBN 978-1-60709-757-0 (pbk. : alk. paper) — ISBN 978-1-60709-758-7 (electronic)
    1. Educational leadership. 2. School management and organization. 3. Curriculum planning. I. Studer, Susan Clark. II. Title.
    LB2805.S5845 2010
    371.2—dc22

                                                                  2010013772

*This book is dedicated to our colleagues
at California Baptist University.*

Contents

Preface   vii

1 Complexity Simplified   1

2 Complexity at Work in the American Educational System   23

3 Leveraging Complexity at the Policy Level   73

4 Leveraging Complexity at the Organizational Level   97

References   125

Index   135

About the Authors   143

Preface

I think the next century will be the century of complexity.

— Stephen Hawking

The challenges of the twenty-first century will require new ways of thinking about and understanding the complex, interconnected and rapidly changing world in which we live and work. And the new field of complexity science is providing the insights we need to push our thinking in new directions.

— Sanders and McCabe (2003, 5)

New paradigms provide innovative perspectives and solutions to old problems. While dominant paradigms have been relatively few over the centuries and have been slow in being replaced, emerging paradigms provide clarity where others have fallen short (Kuhn 1970). Historically, each new paradigm optimistically claimed to be the unified field theory only to be eventually, albeit gradually, confronted with questions it was unable to answer in a manner consistent within the existing framework.

Complexity theory, the study of complex systems, is the newest and most promising dominant paradigm for multiple disciplines. Similar to previous paradigms, complexity science provides a clear, comprehensive, congruent, cohesive, and consistent explanation of particular aspects of reality. Dissimilar to previous paradigms, complexity science explains and predicts diverse phenomena, becoming a paradigm for paradigms. Goldstein (2008) documents how the study of complex systems "represents a confluence of many ideas across from many fields in the sciences

and mathematics that have been developing in many exciting new ways"
(19). Complexity theory emerged as various disciplines independently
and simultaneously recognized that traditional linear explanations were
not sufficient. Complexity science matured as similar self-organizing
patterns were discovered to be at work in both the atomistic and material
traditions practiced in the physical and social sciences.

Evidence of complexity behind the appearance of order began to be
noticed and discussed as a possible new paradigm as early as the 1940s.
The development of electronic technology generated newer and faster
calculations that allowed for a deeper analysis of existing phenomena
(Weaver 1948). A classic example of technology bringing complexity
to the forefront came in 1963 with the work of Edward Lorenz from the
Massachusetts Institute of Technology. Lorenz was experimenting with
computers to predict weather. On one occasion he rounded off the data
that he collected to limit the amount of usage time on, by today's standards, a relatively slow and bulky computer and derived radically unexpected results compared to the previous computer-generated scenarios.
Lorenz had concluded that the significance of rounding off and the radical
differences in weather scenarios that resulted was equivalent to the results
of a butterfly flapping its wings in Brazil setting off a tornado in Texas
(Hilborn 1994). Sanders and McCabe (2003) state:

> In the last twenty years, rapid advances in high-speed computing and
> computer graphics have created a revolution in the scientific understand-
> ing of complex systems. We now have the ability to move beyond the old
> paradigm; to look at whole systems; to study the interactions of many in-
> dependent variables and to explore the underlying principles, structure, and
> dynamics of complex physical, biological, and social systems. (5)

During World War II, as interdisciplinary approaches were adopted to
manage the logistics of getting supplies where they were needed, opera-
tional analyses revealed an interdependency and nonlinear relationship
among variables. The shipment of military supplies required more than
just attention to timetables. It required a coordinated consideration of
communication, weather, equipment maintenance schedules, and staffing
needs, morale, and agendas (Weaver 1948).

At the same time, researchers in the biological and social sciences
were discovering the means by which stability is maintained in social

systems (Jackson 2000). Commencing in 1942, researchers such as Bateson, Mead, and Wiener convened regularly to discuss complexity in the creation and maintenance of biological and social systems (Keeney 1983; Wiener 1948). According to Keeney, participants sensed a new paradigm emerging as they explained how variables are relational and interdependent (versus independent and dependent). The systems approach rightly recognized that behaviors happen in response to feedback in order to achieve relative homeostasis in the system.

Complexity science gained momentum as a cohesive body of evidence and literature was emerging from the physical, biological, and social sciences. Gleick (1987), in his seminal best seller, *Chaos: Making a New Science*, documented and illustrated the latest advancements in complexity science from a variety of disciplines. Gleick's work continues to serve as an introduction to several key concepts of complexity science.

Organizations dedicated to the study and application of complexity science have emerged over the last decades. The Santa Fe Institute, the leading institute dedicated to understanding and applying complexity science to contemporary issues, celebrated twenty years of interdisciplinary studies of complexity science in 2004. In 2002, the U.S. Department of Education commissioned the Washington Center for Complexity and Public Policy to examine how complexity science was being used "with special attention to implications for its use in understanding and influencing the complexities of our educational system" (Sanders and McCabe 2003, 5). The report documented that complexity science had achieved a status of wide application and use.

The American Educational Research Association (AERA) developed a Chaos and Complexity Theory Special Interest Group (SIG) that had its first full meeting at the AERA 1996 Annual Conference. As posted on their website, the purpose of the SIG is "to apply, advance, and extend chaos and complexity theories to inquiry, research, and theory related to educational contexts" (American Educational Research Association 2010).

Books and journals devoted to complexity also emerged at an accelerated rate. Birnbaum (1988) and Morrison (2002) applied complexity theory to educational leadership. Uhl-Bien and Marion (2008) and Marion (1999) utilized complexity science to shed insight on leadership theory and formal social systems. Kiel and Elliott (1997), in their edited book

Chaos Theory in the Social Sciences: Foundations and Application, applied the new paradigm of complexity to political science, economics, and sociology for dynamic insights to particular social phenomena.

Wheatley (1997) attempted to popularize complexity theory by applying the concepts to leadership in her book *Leadership and the New Science: Discovering Order in a Chaotic World.* An international peer-reviewed journal, *Complicity: An International Journal of Complexity and Education,* dedicated to applying complexity science to education, had its inaugural issue in December 2004. *Complicity* provides a comprehensive annotated bibliography on its website for those interested in the additional study of complexity science and as an example of the burgeoning writing on complexity science that is taking place.

The journal *Emergence: Complexity and Organization (E:CO)* debuted in April 2004 as a revised version of the journal *Emergence: A Journal of Complexity Issues in Organizations and Management,* which was launched in 1999. The *E:CO* is published by the Institute for the Study of Coherence and Emergence in association with the Cognitive Edge and the Complexity Society. *E:CO* is "an international and interdisciplinary conversation" for individuals interested in "human organizations as complex systems" and "the implications of complexity science for those organizations." It attempts to blend "the integrity of academic inquiry and the impact of business practice" and "integrate multiple perspectives in management theory, research, practice, and education." The quarterly journal is published in print and online, and its purpose, as stated on the website, is

to bridge three gaps:

- The distance between academic theory and professional practice;
- The space between the mathematics and the metaphors of complexity thinking; and
- The disparity between formal idealizations and actual human organizations.

(Institute for the Study of Coherence and Emergence 2010)

This primer is written with two broad purposes. One purpose is to provide a helpful and succinct introductory overview of complexity theory in order to equip leaders with a user-friendly framework to better lead complex environments. Nothing guides practice better than a good theory rightly understood. Previous writings on complexity tend to retain either an overly technical or mystical language that makes complexity science appear more complex than necessary, or they undermine the utility of complexity theory for understanding hard social realities. This primer uses lay terminology and examples to explain and illustrate the main components of complex and dynamic systems.

A second purpose of this book is to use complexity theory to better understand the nature of policy reform in the American educational system. A systemic perspective provides innovative insights to policy patterns for better policy planning. Ultimately this primer is designed to pick up from where traditional paradigms fail and to equip leaders to optimize performance at both the micro (organizational) and macro (policy) levels of complex environments.

Chapter 1 briefly explains the seven components of complex systems, equipping the reader with the foundational concepts of complexity theory. Chapter 2 provides a brief and systematic history of education in the United States through the lens of complexity theory as an example of complexity at work in the policy environment. The alternative interpretation of educational history and reform illustrates the true nature of the educational pendulum so that leaders can better anticipate and manage future changes associated with the complex environments of schools. Chapter 3 illustrates how educational policy behaves in a predictable pattern consistent with the tenets of complexity science. The reader will gain additional understanding, evidence, and examples of how complexity science can be used to bring about desired outcomes at the policy level of complex environments. Chapter 4 provides specific principles for leaders to make the most of chaos at both the organizational and policy levels. The chapter provides simple guidelines to leverage systemic change to bring about optimal outcomes.

Chapter One

Complexity Simplified

The more complex society gets, the more sophisticated leadership must become. Complexity means change, but specifically it means rapidly occurring, unpredictable, nonlinear change.

—Michael Fullan (2001, ix)

An often-quoted Bible verse states that leadership is a fine work, and those who desire it are to be commended (I Timothy 3:1). Unfortunately, having the desire alone to be a leader is not necessarily sufficient to meet the complex challenges and demands associated with leadership, especially in today's global community. On any given day, leaders constantly manage competing interests, multiple constituents, and bombarding feedback. They need the requisite wisdom on how nature really works in order to develop strategic competencies to succeed in leading people and institutions in the context of complex environments. This book is designed to provide readers with a view of the hidden architecture behind social and physical systems. Equipped with a new paradigm, leaders will be positioned to leverage chaos to bring about realistic and desirable outcomes at the organizational and policy levels.

As noted in the preface, this new and promising paradigm comes from chaos and complexity theory in which "scientists have recently discovered that various complex systems have an underlying architecture governed by shared organizing principles" (Barabasi and Bonabeau 2003, 50). The beauty of complexity is that it describes simply how nature works (Buchanan 2001; Bak 1996), and for that reason it is self-evident and easily recognizable everywhere one looks—once people learn to look for it.

1

Complexity science can appear counterintuitive at first because it describes science and history as nonlinear systems. Current Western civilization and science continuously frame cause and effect, the passage of time, and formal structures in a linear fashion. Because there are regular patterns at work and life unfolds chronologically, it is easy to conclude that life is linear and predictable. However, it will become evident that the regular patterns in life happen as part of larger nonlinear patterns that are governed by universal rules.

The limitation of linear orientation or frame of reference is revealed by the fact that "half the decisions made in business and related organizations fail" (Nutt 2002, 3). Many future outcomes are not predicated on one or two resolutions, but rather a series of seemingly unrelated events that are part of a larger pattern. Complexity theory does not deny that for each action there is a reaction, but rather demonstrates that for each action there are multiple reasons and reactions, some of which are more obvious than others. In a similar fashion, any one problem is not often the direct result of the identified precipitating event, but typically a symptom of something else in which the root cause or multiple root causes may well be five "whys" deep.

Swinton (2009) provides an amusing example of how a root cause analysis solved a pernicious problem confronting many cities.

The local authority was paying a small fortune for cleaning bird droppings from a bronze statue in the central square. First they tried different coatings, each claiming to be easier to clean than the last. Then they tried a noise generator to scare the birds away, but to no avail. Getting more creative with their solutions, a bird of prey was encouraged to live in the central square, but even that couldn't keep the birds away.

One evening the lighting in the square failed and wasn't fixed for 3 days. When the contractor came to fix the fault, he noticed the statue was remarkably clean, which he mentioned to his local authority colleague. "Interesting," thought this smart lady, "I wonder what would happen if . . ." and off she went with a cunning plan. She switched the lights on later in the evening, and the statue remained ever more mess-free.

And how? At dusk, insects were attracted to the bright lights highlighting the esteemed bronze statue. And where insects go, birds go too, hungry for an evening meal. By switching the lights on after dusk, the insects weren't attracted to the square, and the birds went elsewhere for food. Simple!

Save yourself from cleaning up a lot of bird poo by using root cause analysis to solve problems quickly and precisely. (1)

The reason many people do not recognize the simple rules governing complex phenomena is because the dominant reductionist paradigm has conditioned inquiring minds to frame questions and concepts in a traditional linear fashion. Marion (2008) astutely observes that

> the problem is not that complexity is necessarily dense and impenetrable to those not trained in its intricacies; rather, the problem is our frames of reference for understanding get in the way. We tend, for example, to define our experiences in terms of variables and linear cause and effect, reductionism (or analyzing the specific on the assumption that it will reveal the whole), predictability, equilibrium, and linear evolution. (2)

While linear explanations make sense for highly circumscribed social and physical realities, most of life is too complex to be reduced to simple cause and effect relationships. In addition, linear explanations appear to work for many scenarios only because systems emerge with a degree of stability as part of a larger pattern at work. While the variable Y may be the result of X, there are additional variables interacting such that the influences of variables A through W, and even Z, interact with X to yield Y—rarely does X act alone on Y.

The reason for the car accident was not necessarily the driver in the other car (why did the accident happen when it did?), but a combination of factors plus the driver of the other car. While sometimes the precipitating event is the direct cause and proportionate to the outcome, nothing makes sense without the context. A nonlinear orientation asks why did it happen now and not before or later? Nonlinear dynamics and complexity enable thinking outside the box by recognizing the underlying architecture common to complex systems.

Koch (1999) makes a similar observation on the advantage of nonlinear thinking over the traditional reductionist paradigms, noting that

> the last third of the twentieth century has seen a revolution in the way that scientists think about the universe, overturning the prevailing wisdom of the past 350 years. That prevailing wisdom was a machine-based and rational view. . . . All phenomena were reduced to predictable, *linear* relationships.

. . . But in the second half of the twentieth century it seems much more accurate to view the world as an evolving organism where the whole system is more than the sum of its parts, and where relationships between parts are nonlinear. Causes are difficult to pin down, there are complex interdependencies between causes and causes and effects are blurred. The snag with linear thinking is that it doesn't always work, it is an oversimplification of reality. Equilibrium is illusory or fleeting. The universe is wonky. (13)

He adds, "Yet chaos theory, despite its name, does not say that everything is a hopeless and incomprehensible mess. Rather, there is a self-organized logic lurking behind the disorder, a predictable nonlinearity" (13).

This chapter is designed to equip the leader with seven simple principles for understanding the "self-organized logic lurking behind complexity" that seems to manage all dynamic multilinear and nonlinear systems. The goal of this chapter is to provide a foundational understanding of the hidden architecture of complex systems. This chapter serves either as an introduction to first-time readers or as a review for those already familiar with complexity science. Regardless of the previous level of understanding of the theory, this chapter will provide leaders with the essential rules or characteristics found in every complex system in order to strategically initiate and maintain desired outcomes in complex environments.

The following seven concepts are logical extensions of each other and explain why and how dynamic systems function, survive, and even thrive in the midst of chaos:

1. Homeostasis and change
2. Strange attractors
3. Fractals
4. Cybernetics
5. Emergence
6. Sensitive dependence
7. Self-organized criticality

These concepts make the complexity paradigm appear foreboding, highly technical, and even complicated. The paradox of complexity theory is that although it may appear complicated, and even chaotic, the concepts are relatively simple and abound in nature (Buchanan 2001; Morrison 2002).

According to Morrison (2002), the word *complexity* stems from the Latin root "to entwine," meaning that an organism interacts dynamically with its environment, influences it, and in turn, is being influenced by it. The interdependence of variables makes the system dynamic. For example, students do not behave the same every day (even every hour) in school. The time of day, month, and year, subject matter, class activities, fluid peer relations and standings, moods and temperaments of various participants, and even the weather become factors in determining the students' level of engagement and learning moment by moment. The complexity of the classroom is evidenced all the more in that each student brings at least two others along (i.e., two parents, siblings, etc.) every time he or she enters the classroom.

In understanding human development, Peck (1978) makes the observation that it is amazing more things do not go wrong, given all that could go wrong. The complexity paradigm captures this dynamic interdependence that explains why more things do not break down into chaos or why so many things go right in complex systems.

As already mentioned, while complexity is ubiquitous, some systems are more complex than others. Figure 1.1 illustrates that increased levels of complexity are a function of the organizational size, the layers of participants, the number of feedback sources, the speed of feedback, and the levels of demand or diversity upon the particular subsystem. For example, while local governments deal with similar demands at the state and federal government level, the former has fewer numbers of internal and external demands because it services a smaller constituent base and geographical area. On the other hand, state governments have hundreds of local governments to coordinate activities with and the federal government has fifty states to coordinate activities with and between. In the educational setting, while private schools are similar in mission and in structure to public schools, they tend to have less diverse constituents and fewer state and federal requirements. In the business world, small businesses have relatively smaller customer bases to please and suppliers to work with, while national and international businesses have multiple customer bases, suppliers, and distributors to satisfy. Not just size, but the rate in which information flows determines the level of complexity. Advances in technology provide more and faster feedback only to solicit more immediate responses.

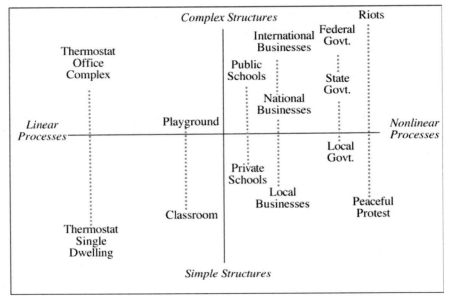

Figure 1.1.

Institutions and activities identified in figure 1.1 are located according to their complexity relative to their respective counterpart(s) and are provided to illustrate why complexity increases within certain systems. The placement of specific institutions and activities in figure 1.1 are not intended to document which systems are more complex overall, but only relative to their respective counterparts. Regardless of the level of complexity, there are simple rules at work in each institution and institutional system. The same rules that cause *major* earthquakes and avalanches, wars, national policy changes, promotions, relational harmony or strife, and even traffic jams are the same that cause *minor* earthquakes and avalanches, riots, local policy changes, career advancement, marital harmony or strife, and traffic congestion.

There is an amazing similarity across scales because common rules are at work. Regardless of the institutional system, complexity science explains these general rules that govern different dynamic systems. Like statistics, complexity science lies at the crossroads of many domains.

Many books and articles have been written on each of the concepts of complexity about to be addressed. The reader is encouraged to pursue additional readings to develop a fuller appreciation of the principles beyond what the following brief descriptions can provide. The following provides an introductory explanation to the seven concepts common to all dynamic systems. The specific components are applied to leadership practices in chapters 3 and 4.

The starting point for our study of the architecture common to all non-linear systems is the illustration of simple complexity shown in figure 1.2. In heating or cooling a single room, a simple thermostat manages slight changes in the environment to maintain the desired equilibrium point of the set temperature. The thermostat operates as a "strange attractor" (the reason for it being "strange" will be explained later) by determining the desired equilibrium point or homeostasis for the temperature of the room. The sensor receives feedback from the environment to ascertain if the set equilibrium point is achieved and maintained. As the temperature of the room heats up because of environmental influences from outside (perhaps a sunny, warm day), a message (feedback) from the thermostat signals the air conditioning for cool air. Once the room temperature reaches the desired state, the thermostat signals the air conditioning to idle. The fluc-tuation of the air conditioner's coming on and off (change) is in response to the thermostat setting (point attractor).

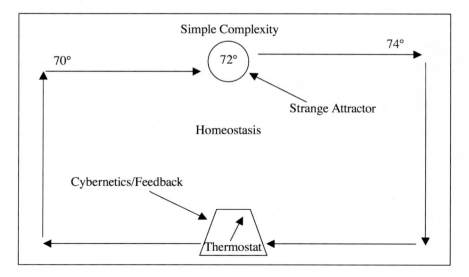

Figure 1.2.

Another example of a simple complex system is the human digestive system. When people are hungry, a signal (feedback) for food intake is sent to the brain. Once the stomach is full (homeostasis) another signal is sent to the brain to stop eating. The degree of satiety is the desired equilibrium point or the strange attractor.

HOMEOSTASIS AND CHANGE

The first notion to master in simple complexity is the twin concepts of change and homeostasis. Equilibrium is established when the system is in balance, no matter how balance is measured. The human body constantly seeks homeostasis or desired levels in temperature, salinity, and acidity. Ecology requires proper balance between the number of species and flora that can be supported in a specific ecosystem. The economy and social systems have an invisible hand (Smith 1776) and invisible circle (de Tocqueville 1835), respectively, that determines the range of acceptable behaviors. As illustrated in figure 1.2, equilibrium is defined as anything between 70° and 74°F.

Change is the twin concept to equilibrium. Equilibrium does not exist unless there is change. Systems are always changing in order to remain the same (i.e., the more things change, the more they stay the same—a French proverb). In the example of temperature comfort, the air conditioner is repeatedly turning off and on (change) to maintain equilibrium. People eat and stop eating (change) to maintain a desired state of satisfaction. Policies are constantly introduced to correct or compensate for a system approaching an imbalance (more details in chapter 3). The same is found in social systems. For example, children receive more and less discipline (change) as a function of the desired behavioral patterns (equilibrium).

An illustration of simple rules at work in the complexity of a family situation is when the teenager who historically has been an A student starts to earn Fs. The parents who have recently had a major advancement in their careers adjust their schedules to return to the level of involvement they once had when their child was earning As. Sure enough, the teenager's grades soon return to the A level. Once the As are secured, the parents, believing all is now well, readjust to the demands of their new careers. Soon, the student's grades return to the F range, resulting in the parents providing extra attention to their child.

The child is sending feedback (indirect as it is) that the parents' level of involvement and engagement prior to their promotions was the preferred state of equilibrium. The parents had a desired equilibrium point for their student's academic performance and adjusted (changed) their behavior in order to maintain that homeostasis. Eventually the parents realize what their child is missing and needing, and with some intentionality, can maintain the expectations (strange attractors) of both family and work.

Figure 1.2 illustrates simple complexity because it has only one strange attractor, or what is called a "point attractor." Imagine how the complexity increases as the number of strange attractors increase. A family system with multiple children, to achieve balance, has to compete against work schedules and demands, individual interests and needs of each member, and financial constraints.

Teachers in any given classroom are called to balance multiple strange attractors. For the most part, students are prone to socialize while teachers are prone to teach (Cusick 1992). Learning cannot take place unless there is some type of classroom order. At the same time, if there is too much classroom control, teaching defaults to rote learning and exercises. Good teaching is maintaining a fluid balance between order and learning by continually reigning in or loosening the reigns of control to meet the various expectations for learning and order that teachers inherit from students, peers, administration, parents, and the community.

In a classroom and in a democracy, the competing demands of excellence, equality, choice, and efficiency act as powerful strange attractors in legitimizing specific policies and practices (see figure 1.3). As elaborated in chapters 2 and 3, parents, teachers, administrators, and politicians strive for balance between these equally important values.

For the most part, however, maintaining point equilibrium is a dynamic process. While the body maintains 98.6 degrees Fahrenheit, temperature fluctuations outside cause the metabolism to either increase or decrease in order to regulate the body temperature. The body's metabolism is always changing to maintain 98.6 degrees. When a child's mobile is swinging, it can only swing so far until it self-corrects only to undergo another self-correction until it eventually reaches the desired state of rest. As with the illustration in figure 1.2, the changes from the outside environment require the thermostat to signal minor changes in order to maintain the equilibrium of the desired temperature.

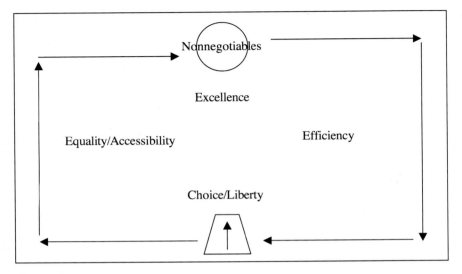

Figure 1.3.

As the system matures (emerges) and attains sustainability, it retains essential structures that give the system its unique characteristics. These structures make the system relatively stable and resilient over time. Leaders do well to judiciously anticipate and welcome change as a means to maintain stability. Additional leadership practices associated with the features of complex systems will be presented in chapter 4.

STRANGE ATTRACTORS

The equilibrium points are determined by what were initially called strange attractors, and are now commonly referred to as dynamic attractors and repellers (recognizing that dynamic forces are not always attractive). The attractors were called strange because the "force" was not necessarily tangible and it was the pattern that revealed an attraction (or repellent) in the system. Gleick (1987) demonstrates "one of the most powerful inventions of modern science" was that a "strange attractor lives in phase space" (134). According to Gleick,

> In phase space the complete state of knowledge about a dynamical system at a single instant in time collapses to a point. That point is the dynamical

system—at that instant. At the next instant, though, the system will have changed, ever so slightly, and so the point moves. The history of the system can be charted by the moving point, tracing its orbit through phase space with the passage of time. (134)

Another way to understand a strange attractor is that it is a point in the system where the pattern will eventually end up at any point in time, whether from an attraction or repellant in the system. In figure 1.2, the thermostat behaves like a strange attractor in the sense that it calls the temperature back into balance in response to environmental fluctuations. Strange attractors maintain population and weather patterns. While the weather predictions are not always accurate on a daily basis, they perform extremely well on average. The norms and values of the macro and micro social systems serve as strange attractors.

As will be elaborated on in chapters 2 and 3, the reason educational reform is continuous and repeats itself (the educational pendulum) is because of the various strange attractors (competing values) in the educational system. Formal leaders are strange attractors for their organization, albeit not the only strange attractors, nor the only leaders. It is what leaders attend to and how they attend to it that gets mirrored throughout the organization and becomes the point at which equilibrium is established.

Logically it follows that the greater the number of strange attractors in the system, the more complex the system becomes. For example, a family with one child is less chaotic than a family with five children. The federal government has many more constituents with competing demands than state governments, and state governments have more demands than local governments. Complexity increases, not just from an increase in the number of players, but from the variety of expectations represented in the system. Private universities that serve a more homogenous population tend to be less complex than public universities of comparable size that serve a more heterogeneous population. The diversity of expectations is one of the factors that determines the level of complexity, as illustrated in figure 1.1.

Leaders would do well to establish their fluid hierarchy of nonnegotiables (dominant values) that will govern their practices. Establishing the parameters of what is preferred and allowable equips leaders to manage ambiguity and delineate an acceptable range of options in which to operate.

FRACTALS

Despite the various levels of complexity among comparable organizations, there is an amazing amount of similarity across scales. While politicians at the federal, state, and local levels play by similar rules, or have similar strange attractors, the scale varies. This similarity across scales reveals a much to be admired functional symmetry throughout the system.

Similarity across scales is another concept of complexity science that is a logical extension of strange attractors and homeostasis. The patterns that emerge at the macro level because of the strange attractors are mirrored throughout the micro levels of the system and vice versa. Basically, in dynamic systems, subsets take on the features of the whole in what are known as fractals. The most recognized fractals belong to the Mandelbrot set named after the father of fractals, Benoit Mandelbrot. Fractals are the reiterations of patterns across scales in a system. Self-similar patterns are found in nature and social groupings. Family units, regardless of social economic status or country of origin, share similar characteristics while retaining features that distinguish each family unit as unique. It is the same with schools and corporate headquarters. While schools and business offices are easily recognizable because of common corresponding features, each school and corporate structure and culture are uniquely different.

A classic example of symmetry across scales is the story of David and Goliath in the Bible. David used the similar skills and confidence that he developed and used in protecting his sheep that were being killed by lions and bears to slay a giant. The skill of killing a lion by using a slingshot is the same skill as killing a giant; it is the scale that varies. Organizations promote people with proven skills to positions where relatively the same skill sets are needed, just the level of complexity (or scale) increases. This is one reason why people who can manage ambiguity and complexity and adapt are promoted over those who lack such ability even though they share the same technical skill sets (Leslie and Velsor 1996; Friedman 2005).

Leaders need to be sensitive to the fact that their standards and idiosyncrasies (both positive and negative) get mirrored throughout their organization. Leaders who model and reinforce punctuality will see their subordinates take punctuality seriously and, subsequently, expect punctuality from their respective subordinates. Whether it is punctuality, certain standards of excellence, or styles of relating, the dominant values will mirror themselves throughout the system to become essential features of the system.

As the strange attractors determine relative equilibrium points for the system and eventually mirror themselves throughout the system, in order for equilibrium to be maintained, a mechanism is needed to sense disequilibrium—disturbances or changes in the system. This ushers in the fourth key principle in complexity science, feedback, or what is known as cybernetics.

CYBERNETICS

Cybernetics is the word of choice for feedback among complexity aficionados. Cybernetics, while used by Plato, was popularized by Norbert Wiener in 1948 with his book *Cybernetics*. Plato, and Ampere (1834), used the term to discuss the science of government and the activity of the "governor" as steering the community. Wiener used the metaphor of cybernetics to describe communication and control of animals and machines.

The word *cybernetics* is a transliteration of the Greek word Κυβευήτης (*kubernites*) and literally means steersman. The individual staffing the rudder of a ship is constantly making minor midcourse corrections to keep the ship headed toward its destination; the more the steersman adjusts the rudder (change) the better able to stay the course (remain the same). Just as the stronger currents or winds require the steersman to make more changes, complex environments require the skilled steersman to respond to the many competing demands.

Cybernetics is feedback that is heeded or the means in which the system regulates itself (versus feedback that is random or "just noise"). Self-regulating systems have sensors tuned for specific types of feedback in order to make requisite adaptations consistent with the expectations of the strange attractors in the system. Wiener (1948) used the concept of cybernetics to develop automatic range finders for antiaircraft guns.

Cybernetics is also the principle behind guided missile technology. A guided missile's trajectory makes constant minor midcourse corrections as it is en route to the designated target in order to stay on course—again, the concept that the more the trajectory of the missile self-corrects (changes), the more the trajectory stays on course (stays the same). The midcourse corrections are recalibrations of the missile's trajectory based upon the feedback that is received as the missile travels. Systems can experience much feedback, but if the feedback is not sensed, or sensed and not used, then the feedback is just noise and serves no self-regulatory function.

All dynamic systems are cybernetic in that they are self-regulating and dependent upon feedback to perform, constrained, or driven by the strange attractors at work. The importance of feedback for the survival of the family unit, one of the most basic dynamic social systems, is evident in the frequency of communication required to coordinate activities of the various members of the household.

In addition, when a family enjoys rich social capital, additional feedback is informative and timely. A child's teachers, neighborhood friends, and extended family are positioned to provide insights to parents that they would not otherwise have. Both authors remember the need to behave in school or at a friend's house, knowing any news of misbehavior would reach their respective parents prior to returning home. The various feedback mechanisms were used to establish and maintain expectations of behavior in and out of the home. The system works well when feedback is sought out and used.

At the same time, not all feedback is treated equally. Some parents minimize, if not react harshly against, any corrective feedback from teachers that reflects negatively on their child. Lest they be attacked or unduly criticized by zealous parents for providing candid feedback on their students' progress, many teachers have been conditioned to abdicate the once valued role of *in loco parentis* in response to parents behaving badly (Gibbs 2005). Unfortunately, the loss of such social capital undermines the contribution of the village in raising children.

Leaders do well to build mechanisms to judiciously solicit and provide feedback so that the right behaviors and judgments emerge. Leaders do exceptionally well when they actively listen, often the most difficult aspect of communication.

EMERGENCE

Like flowers that grow in the direction of the sun, systems grow (or emerge) in the direction of their feedback. Heylighen and Joslyn (1992) provide the following brief overview of emergence in systems theory on Principia Cybernetica (a website dedicated to disseminating papers and research on complexity):

> Systems theory was proposed in the 1940's by the biologist Ludwig von Bertalanffy *(General Systems Theory, 1968)*, and furthered by Ross Ashby *(Introduction to Cybernetics*, 1956). Von Bertalanffy was both reacting against reductionism and attempting to revive the unity of science. He emphasized that real systems are open to, and interact with, their environments, and that they can acquire qualitatively new properties through emergence, resulting in continual evolution. Rather than reducing an entity (e.g., the human body) to the properties of its parts or elements (e.g., organs or cells), systems theory focuses on the arrangement of and relations between the parts relative to the whole (cf. holism). This particular organization determines a system, which is independent of the concrete substance of the elements (e.g., particles, cells, transistors, people, etc). Thus, the same concepts and principles of organization underlie the different disciplines (physics, biology, technology, sociology, etc.), providing a basis for their unification. Systems concepts include: system-environment boundary, input, output, process, state, hierarchy, goal-directedness, and information. (1)

A system consists of interdependent parts working together for desired outcomes as defined by its respective boundaries or parameters established by the strange attractors. Systems emerge as the sum of the parts becomes greater than the individual parts by themselves. For example, the human body is one system comprising many subsystems (i.e., respiratory, circulatory, digestive, endocrine, neurological systems). A social system is defined by its members and their specific mores and customs. The norms, or patterns of relating, are established as a means of keeping the family unit intact according to shared expectations. Whether dysfunctional or functional, patterns of relating are established and maintained as they become reinforced and eventually entrenched in the family system. The first day of school sets precedents as to what behavior is acceptable or not and sets the tone for the whole year.

Social groups at work and play have unstated assumptions and group norms regarding work ethic, punctuality, appropriate and inappropriate humor, fiscal conservativeness, and so on. Norms emerge over time as nonnegotiables are established. A new employee typically is wise to figure out (even prior to employment) what are the assumptions and norms for group performance; what happens if an employee is late, or leaves early, or right at 5 p.m. These group norms emerge via subtle and not so subtle messages in the environment. Group norms establish rules of engagement. A supervisor who is the first to arrive and the last to leave creates a different culture than one who is the last to arrive and the first to leave. A supervisor who uses gentle words to hold people accountable creates a different culture than one who uses harsh words. What leaders attend to and how they attend to people and projects matters.

Complexity and systems theories also explain how bad company corrupts good morals. Social groups form and establish a set of assumptions and norms of what is acceptable and not acceptable. A new member in the group throws the system temporarily into disequilibrium. If a new group member is not in harmony with the existing norms (or strange attractors), then either the norms of the group adjust, the new member adjusts to the group, or the new member disengages from the group.

For example, if a peer group stands for purity in language and abstinence from drugs and alcohol, they will be selective in who is included or not in the group. However, the desire to be friendly and inclusive is also a strange attractor for the group, so that a degree of tolerance is embraced to welcome potential members. Those who join the group and participate in the particular vices familiarize the group to the vices in question. At that point, the group is at risk of being "renormed" as familiarity with the particular vices breeds tolerance and the subsequent and gradual acceptance of the particular vices is introduced into the group. Unless other things happen, over time what was anathema to the group becomes socially acceptable.

Many people addicted to drugs did not wake up one day to say, "I think I will become addicted to drugs." The typical story is that while they thought they would never do drugs, a friend prompted them to "just try it." The new beginning sets in motion a new pattern. Granted, there are many people who take one puff and stop, but in that case there were certain things in place that precluded an addictive lifestyle from emerging, while in the previous scenario there were other things at work that gave way for an addictive lifestyle to happen.

People do what they do because somehow it is reinforcing, or it works for them, eventually developing routines of behaviors that become ingrained habits. For example, no one wakes up and decides to become an alcoholic. It is a process that emerges over time. The first drink can be so soothing after a difficult day at work that drinks are sought out on a regular basis to pacify stress. The alcoholic emerges if and when some desired state of harmony (equilibrium) is established in the system. It is not uncommon for people or the system to enable a person's chronic drinking as a calm drunk may be preferred over a sober hothead, or an angry drunk perceived better than an absentee provider.

Neural development is another classic example of emerging systems. Neural pathways develop over time after repeated use, based upon the types of initial stimulation received. Eventually the pathways become preferred routes that lead to stimulation-seeking behavior (this is the premise of physiological addictions). Another classic example is the development of the Internet. It emerged into a World Wide Web because of what it did, far from what the innovators ever intended the Internet to do and be when it was created.

The American public education system was not devised from a grand master plan, but evolved over time as a result of competing forces to make it what it is today, different from what other countries have to offer, all dependent on unique initial conditions. Ant hills, flocking behavior, weather patterns, ecologies, river systems, group dynamics, and neonatal development emerge to become self-organized and survive with relative consistency over time.

Leaders do well to vigilantly buffer and nurture the system so that the right patterns emerge consistent with the system's dominant values. As systemic thinkers, leaders also do well to anticipate the intended and unintended consequences of their decisions.

SENSITIVE DEPENDENCE

Eventually what emerges is contingent upon the starting points in what is referred to as sensitive dependency on initial conditions. While the patterns emerge in the direction of the feedback, the impetus for systems to emerge is a function of the interactions between initial variables and existing conditions. It is these initial conditions that imprint the system and give the system its unique essence and characteristics.

As mentioned in the preface, Edward Lorenz documented the sensitive dependency on initial conditions in his use of computers to forecast the weather. Computers in the 1960s were large and slow. To save on computer time Lorenz rounded off the data and derived radically unexpected results from when he entered the original start data at the front end of the calculations. At first, thinking there was computer error, Lorenz eventually concluded that the rounding off reflected the sensitive temperament of the system or what became known as the "butterfly effect." The significance of rounding off and the radical differences in weather scenarios that resulted was reportedly the equivalent of a butterfly flapping its wings in Brazil setting off a tornado in Texas (Hilborn 1994).

Basically, sensitive dependence recognizes that a small change can lead to a big effect(s). Gladwell (2002) in his book *The Tipping Point: How Little Things Can Make a Big Difference* documents and illustrates how various social phenomena emerge from small events because of the simple rules at work in the particular system. Group dynamics can change drastically with the introduction of a certain type of new member. A rainy day can transform relatively routinized classroom dynamics. One person refusing to give up her seat on a bus can be a catalyst for major civil rights reform. An encouraging word or smile can transform a person's day. Sensitive dependence recognizes key leverage points that the system is especially responsive to for maintaining or changing the system. Leaders are catalysts for change. Leaders who know their system well are positioned to judiciously leverage critical features for disproportionate results.

SELF-ORGANIZED CRITICALITY

Dynamic systems emerge and adapt to the environment. Simple rules develop to ensure survivability. Strange attractors emerge from what is considered important or essential characteristics for surviving. Feedback is essential for self-correction to take place, consistent with the strange attractors at work. As the system matures, it grows in the direction of the feedback; hence the system emerges toward what is considered important. Patterns for performance develop and are constantly interacting with the environment. It is this interaction with the environment that makes the system relatively stable and temperamental at the same time, or what is known as self-organized criticality. The question then arises as to how it is that a trigger event can be relatively innocuous at one point in time and transformational at another?

Relevant variables interact in the right combination at the right moment to yield outcomes unique to the time and place. For example, while World War I can be traced to the vulnerabilities and tensions at the time of the assassination of Archduke Franz Ferdinand (heir apparent to the Austro-Hungarian throne) in Sarajevo on June 28, 1914, the wrong turn of Ferdinand's chauffeur into the coincidental path of a would-be assassin reveals how temperamental the situation was (Buchanan 2001). How was it that a wrong turn could usher new rules of engagement that gave way to World War I at the time it did?

Sensitive dependence is in part predicated on how systems are organized. The interdependence of parts makes the system organized as if always in a critical state. As mentioned earlier, self-organized criticality exists because the same rules that cause major earthquakes and avalanches, wars, national policy changes, promotions, relational harmony or strife, and even traffic jams are the same that cause minor earthquakes and avalanches, riots, local policy changes, career advancement, marital harmony or strife, and traffic congestion. What determines the triggering of a large-scale change is the timing and relationship of the variables to one another. In complexity science, independent variables are in essence relational and interdependent.

Bak (1996) illustrates self-organized criticality through the metaphor of a sand pile. As sand is trickled downward and the pile builds, most of the time there will be a number of small avalanches at certain points and a few large avalanches over time. The larger avalanches will be much less frequent than the smaller avalanches. What determines if the avalanche is small or large is not the rate of the sand falling, but rather the relation of each grain of sand relative to other grains of sand at any one point of time.

Most of the time when a few grains of sand avalanche only the surrounding area is affected. At times though, larger avalanches are triggered because of the history of the situation prior to the larger avalanche. For example, one grain of sand called X (of course hyperbole is being used to illustrate the point) is holding back five grains of sand of which one of the five is holding back ten grains of sand. When the one grain X gives way, not only do the five immediate grains give way, they are now joined by the other ten grains.

This is the same principle behind the old adage of the straw that broke the camel's back. It really wasn't the *one* straw that broke the back, but a combination of the straw and everything else (the history) on the back at that particular time that caused the camel's back to collapse. Self-organized criticality explains why several phenomena operate under what are called power laws. For example, there are a few large corporations relative to the number of small businesses, a few megacities relative to the number of small towns, a few people with millions of dollars relative to the many with only thousands. The power laws are seen even in Internet traffic, with a few sites getting multitudes of hits every day relative to the majority of sites getting a few hits per week. Earthquakes with twice the power are four times as rare. For any city size, there are one-quarter as many cities at twice the size (Adamic 2000; Buchanan 2001).

The power laws are evident in economics, with periods of major depression or boom few in number relative to the number of recessions or economic prosperity. The number of labor strikes is relatively few compared to the number of controversial labor negotiations. The number of riots is relatively few compared to the frequency of skirmishes that occur. What determines the magnitude of the change is the immediate history. Self-organized criticality encourages leaders to prepare for the worst and plan for the best.

Self-organized criticality also acknowledges that complex systems exist at the edge of chaos and could give way to disorder at any point in time under specific conditions. While most perturbations to the system are assimilated, some perturbations have a transformational effect—chaos or bifurcation (the system splits). Wars are the extreme example of a system giving way to chaos. The unbridled power of a world leader can led to chaos and massive destruction, evidenced by Germany's aggression in World War II. At the end of World War II, Germany was initially divided into four zones and temporarily morphed into an East and West Germany. Divorce situations involving children is a classic example of a complex system giving way to transitional chaos to eventually emerge with two parallel systems. One family system becomes two independent systems that retain some similarities to the original system.

SUMMARY AND CONCLUSION

By way of review, the common factors in complex dynamic systems include

1. Homeostasis (and change)
2. Strange attractors
3. Fractals
4. Cybernetics
5. Emergence
6. Sensitive dependence
7. Self-organized criticality

   The more systems change, the more they stay the same; hovering around desired equilibrium points. The strange attractors determine the equilibrium points and mirror themselves throughout the various levels of the system in the form of fractals. Cybernetics is the process in which the system emerges and maintains equilibrium. The system, while relatively stable over time, is vulnerable to small changes having big effects, in part because of sensitive dependence on initial conditions and self-organized criticality (timing and history).

   Because of the relative stability of most systems, the world can easily appear linear. The railroad industry appears linear (literally and theoretically) in keeping the trains on time and on track. Yet, behind the scenes there is so much coordination of loading and unloading schedules, regular maintenance, and upkeep, that without such intensive coordination, chaos would happen. Complexity theory explains how relative stability can exist at the edge of chaos.

   Leaders who understand the rules that govern dynamic social systems are skilled enough in the nuances of systems to lead with wisdom—leading from the metanarrative or big picture. Chapters 2 and 3 apply the seven features of complex adaptive systems to the history of education in the United States. Both chapters demonstrate the utility of complexity theory to provide nontraditional insights into America's educational system and other policy environments. Educational policy and reform do not necessarily stem from rational planning alone, but rather are the outcome of competing values and a function of timing in a dynamic, nonlinear, and emerging system. Chapter 4 examines how the respective implications of the various characteristics of complex systems can be leveraged by leaders to bring about optimal change at the organizational and policy levels.

Chapter Two

Complexity at Work in the American Educational System

It is impossible to predict the time and progress of revolution. It is governed by its own more or less mysterious laws. But when it comes, it moves irresistibly.

—Vladimir Lenin

This chapter provides a detailed, and yet brief, history of the United States' educational system. There are several reasons for utilizing the history of education as the lens to illustrate the architectural rules governing different policy environments versus the history of business, government, public administration, or any other history. Education is one of the more complex professions. Education is much more value-laden in both the outcomes and means when compared to most other professions because of its multiple, and at times, competing soft goals and methods.

Is the purpose of education solely to transmit knowledge, and if so, what knowledge and how much? Should every student be able to cite Shakespeare or Cicero, perform basic algebraic equations, understand the principles of chemistry and physics, and embrace religious and moral traditions, and if so, to what level? Once it is decided what and how much to teach and not to teach, the question becomes: What is the best method for getting students to learn history, math, science, and ethics?

In addition to transferring knowledge, education intentionally and unintentionally socializes students toward dominant values and dispositions. Even the simplest act of hand-raising inculcates an appreciation for respect and the rules of the queue (Hansen 1993). Students are socialized not only by what is taught (and not taught), but by how lessons are taught. What a teacher emphasizes, rewards, and punishes leaves indelible impressions, such that the hidden curriculum often carries more weight than the official and tested curricula. In contrast, the purpose of business is relatively straightforward and tangible. The means to maximizing profit is also tangible and restricted to few options. There is one most efficient means to assemble an automobile while there are multiple means and purposes in educating a child. Compounding the complexity is that while each brand of automobile is technically the same, each child is uniquely different. If one can understand how the educational system works, he or she is well positioned to understand how other systems work.

Education is also offered as the foil because if there were ever a policy with greater implications, it is education. The stakes are too high for the system to be misunderstood. Educational policy impacts everyone, making everybody a constituent with invested interest in the process and outcomes. The following succinct history of education attempts to provide a minimal understanding of the essence of the system, lest various constituents inadvertently do more harm than good in their well-intended involvement.

History is often portrayed in a traditional linear model. While history is chronological, a strictly linear presentation reinforces the false reductionist paradigm that the events of today and tomorrow are the result of yesterday's events. Complexity reveals history as another version of the present and future. A long-term perspective on history reveals patterns are at work in the universe. History cannot help but repeat itself, not because people are forgetful or ignorant of the past, but because the dominant values at work in the past are at work in both the present and future.

A nonlinear history of education is offered as a template to better understand both complexity theory and the unique essence of the educational system. The hope is that a more accurate description of the educational system will drive more realistic educational policy and reform initiatives. In addition, the stories of educational policy reforms are didactic for other policy arenas in demonstrating that policies emerge and adapt (emergence, change, homeostasis) as reiterations (fractals) of precedents (sensitive dependency on initial conditions), as a function of the timing (butterfly effect, self-organized criticality), competing voices (feedback), and competing values (strange attractors).

The following portrayal of system-shaping educational reforms is provided to expose the hidden architecture at the macro level, made obvious once the totality of the individual reforms are understood in relation to each other. The reader is encouraged to remember that as the various reforms identified below are presented, each reform has its own story of complexity and is a reiteration of already established themes and patterns at work on the larger scale. Historical understanding reveals the major patterns and strange attractors influencing both the present and future. The past is the prelude to existing and emerging patterns. Complexity science reinforces the notion that history is didactic when it comes to designing and improving any system.

IN THE BEGINNING—STRANGE ATTRACTORS AND SENSITIVE DEPENDENCE ON INITIAL CONDITIONS

The official beginning of the American educational system is located in the values that led to the founding of the country (the beginning can be found even earlier in history, but for the sake of brevity, this history will begin with the earliest European settlements). The pursuit of individual liberties and a better life brought people to a new continent. Excellence, equality, and freedom were the driving and defining principles of the nascent nation. The values of excellence, equality, and choice would imprint themselves in one form or another in events and institutions that would follow.

In the settlers' quest for a better life based upon principles of liberty, conditions eventually emerged for independence to be declared on July 4, 1776. A high percentage of the people sought the right to be "free and independent" from a tyrannical government. Under the natural laws of "certain unalienable rights," the new nation declared independence for "life, liberty and the pursuit of happiness."

As the nation emerged victorious in its quest for independence, the logical progress was to institute "a more perfect" form of government that would promote and protect its prized values of liberty and equality. On September 17, 1787, representatives for the people of the United States "in order to form a more perfect union, establish justice, insure domestic tranquility, provide for the common defense, promote the general welfare, and secure the blessings of liberty" for themselves and their posterity ordained and established the Constitution of the United States of America.

Two years later on September 25, 1789, an additional ten amendments to the Constitution further solidified certain inalienable rights under the banners of liberty and equality. The Bill of Rights was a logical extension of the processes set in motion by the Declaration of Independence and the Constitution of America. Individuals were now formally free to pursue an excellent life as they saw fit, legitimizing excellence, equality, and liberty as defining values of American life.

The values are codified in the founding documents of the country and serve as the strange attractors governing the emerging educational system. Even though there was intentionally no mention of education in the U.S. Constitution, the founders of the country established an educational system for posterity. From the beginning, the quest for freedom and a better life was predicated on a quality education. An early commitment to education was evident by the founding of the first public-private school in the colonies in 1635 (the Boston Latin School, which is still operating today, making it the oldest public school in the nation) and nine universities prior to the signing of the Declaration of Independence, beginning with Harvard in 1636 (see table 2.1).

This commitment to excellence, manifested in the number of institutions of higher learning established, yielded men of scholarly ability to

Table 2.1. Colleges Established Prior to the Signing of the Declaration of Independence

Date	Original Name	Religious Affiliation	Name Today
1636	Harvard College	Congregational	Same
1693	College of William and Mary	Anglican	Same
1701	Collegiate School at New Haven	Congregational	Yale
1740	The College of Philadelphia	Nonsectarian	University of Pennsylvania
1746	College of New Jersey	Presbyterian	Princeton
1754	King's College	Nonsectarian	Columbia University
1764	College of Rhode Island	Baptist	Brown University
1766	Queen's College	Dutch Reformed	Rutgers University
1769	Dartmouth College	Congregational	Same

Note: Table created from dates and names cited by Lucas (1994).

produce documents such as the Declaration of Independence and the Constitution of the United States. This commitment to excellence and the eventual role education was to play in America's emerging future is articulated in the plaque just outside the Johnston Gate at the Harvard Yard that reads,

> After God had carried us safe to New England
> and we had built our houses,
> provided necessaries for our livelihood,
> reared convenient places for God's worship,
> and settled the civil government,
> one of the next things we longed for
> and looked after was to advance learning
> and perpetuate it to posterity,
> dreading to leave an illiterate ministry
> to the churches when our present ministers
> shall lie in the dust. (Beale 1998, 89)

This same commitment to education paving the way for excellence and a better life led to compulsory education laws (not to be confused with compulsory school laws) as early as 1642 and 1647. The 1642 law required that Massachusetts children and apprentices should be able to read and have knowledge of the common laws. In addition, "all masters of family" were to catechize their children and servants in the principles of religion and secure proper apprenticeship in some "honest and lawful calling."

The law underscored the intrusive role of the community in requiring parents to assume the primary responsibility for the education and welfare of their children. It also empowered colony authorities to intervene in family matters when it seemed to be in the best interest of the community, and supposedly the child. It was the duty of the parents, the court ordered, to teach their own children and if they did not they could be fined or have their children physically removed from their households to become apprentices under the servitude of others. In Plymouth Colony, the colonists viewed it as the family's responsibility, particularly the father, to direct the child's education. If the family proved incapable or unwilling to fulfill its responsibilities, outside authorities were prepared to step in as surrogate parents (Gaither 2008; Jernegan 1918).

A formal system of compulsory education was legally established setting precedent for other colonies. Similar laws were passed in surrounding
colonies, so that by "1671 all of the territory of New England, with the
exception of Rhode Island, was under a system of compulsory education"
(Jernegan 1918, 749).

In 1647, Massachusetts passed a law requiring towns of fifty families
to hire a schoolmaster to educate the children in reading and writing.
Towns of one hundred families were required to hire a grammar school
master who would prepare candidates for Harvard. This commitment to
excellence was now tempered with economy of scales. While there were
regional variations (areas explored by Spain were establishing Franciscan
and Jesuit missions in Florida, New Mexico, Texas, Arizona, and eventually the California coast) in terms of the type and amount of education, the
early establishment of schools demonstrated that commitment to excellence balanced against efficiency (Urban andWagoner 2004).

As evident from the Massachusetts education laws, while the state assumed a limited role in the education of the youth, it was still in the hands
of the parents and local community to prescribe the individual curriculum.
This position was consistent with the lengthy section in Smith's 1776 treatise, *The Wealth of Nations*, that dealt with education. According to Smith,
"public" education was at its best as a joint venture between governing
authorities and individuals (not the monopoly it is today). Smith argued
that the education of youth is a worthwhile enterprise requiring a minimal
level of governmental involvement (primarily in the form of financial
subsidies). In a voucher-like system, excellence in education would be
secured when parents are empowered to choose the different educational
outcomes and experiences.

While Smith was ultimately appealing to a market model of education
as a more efficient and effective means for achieving success, he legitimized the value of individual choice (liberty of conscience) in pursuing
educational ends. For Smith, choice in education encourages emulation
and excellent teaching to survive over mediocrity. Smith articulated well
that the state needs to subsidize education to provide a public good for the
masses of students without taking control away from the parents.

Even though Smith (1776) was writing from across the pond, his message resonated with the zeitgeist of the new country in advancing liberty.
As the country expanded west, the leaders remained committed to pro-

moting excellence, liberty, and equality as efficiently as possible via education. It was common in the early years for state funding of education to be used to supplement students' education, regardless if it was in a private or church-related school. For example, in 1795 the New York "legislature appropriated $50,000 annually for five years as matching funds for towns which set up their own schools. . . . In New York City, however, the state money from the Act of 1795 was not used to create free public schools, but was released instead to support the ten existing church schools and the African Free School" (Ravitch 2000, 7).

At the same time, the existing state and locally supported neighborhood sectarian schools could not accommodate the growing influx of students. As a result, government schools gradually began to emerge. The first free public school in New York City was originally a private philanthropic enterprise. Leading civic business leaders established the "Society for Establishing a Free School in the City of New York, for the education of such poor children as do not belong to, or are not provided for, by any religious society" (Ravitch 2000, 9).

The 1785 Land Ordinance and 1787 Northwest Ordinance acts also made no distinction in funding government-run schools versus other schools open to the public. While the country was still under the Articles of Confederation and precluded from levying taxes, the Land Ordinance Act of 1785 required that the territory outside the original thirteen colonies be divided and sold into townships of six miles square and be made available for public sale as long as "there shall be reserved the lot N 16, of every township, for the maintenance of public schools, within the said township."

The Northwest Ordinance Act of 1787 allowed for lands west of the original colonies to become U.S. territories and eventual states. As new territories and states emerged, article 3 of the Northwest Ordinance Act specifically stated, "Religion, morality, and knowledge, being necessary to good government and the happiness of mankind, schools and the means of education shall forever be encouraged." Public education in the form of government and private schools was promoted and funded early on as the means to build the emerging nation and promote excellence.

The values of excellence, equality, and liberty were foundational to America's identity and became inextricably tied to the educational system. While their lasting imprint on education was strong because education mirrors the dominant values of the larger system, the imprint was solidified when formal education was the means to build and sustain the nation. New demands would emerge as the nation matured, placing corresponding challenges on the educational system.

THE EMERGENCE OF A ONE BEST SYSTEM

Industrialization ushered in the relocation of people from both abroad and the surrounding rural communities to the cities, resulting in swollen villages. Cities were now challenged with educating masses of illiterate children who otherwise would have been working on the farm. Free "public" schools sponsored by philanthropic enterprises were emerging in large cities to educate the masses of students who could not afford an education and would otherwise be on the streets of these urban centers. An affordable method of instruction was needed to school the growing masses of displaced youth. Such a method was found in the Lancastrian monitorial system that "provided education at so low a cost that it made the education of all for the first time seem possible" (Cubberly 1920, 663).

Joseph Lancaster provided England a model of instruction that assigned a pupil to monitor each row of students. The teacher would instruct the monitors who in turn would instruct the students assigned to their respective rows. Classrooms were such that "one teacher, assisted by a number of the brighter pupils whom they designated as monitors, could teach from two hundred to a thousand pupils in one school" (Cubberly 1920, 627).

The first monitorial school on U.S. soil opened in New York City in 1806 and quickly spread to other cities (Cubberly 1920). In a factory-like setting, hundreds of students could learn their spelling, arithmetic, reading, and catechisms with factory-like precision under one teacher and with one book (Lancaster 1805). Education for the masses was now seen as affordable and the issue of classroom size would continue to plague a public system of education with limited resources.

The Lancaster model grew in popularity because it resonated with the virtue of efficiency associated with the Industrial Revolution. The Industrial Revolution introduced systematic and efficient production such that what was good for business was now considered good for education. The factory model for education was institutionalized in the American educational system as standardization of curriculum and gradation of schools (assigning students en masse to grades by age level versus achievement level) were instituted under the rubric of efficiency. Superintendents of factories became the model for education, justifying the need to have superintendents of schools.

The factory model was further solidified with the creation of mammoth school buildings with expansive classrooms arranged off large hallways. These "egg-crate" schools would efficiently accommodate the massive flow of student traffic to and from the grade-level classrooms. Like the factory, a bell coordinated the main activities. Instruction was governed by a bell. The first egg-crate school appeared in 1848 in Boston to eventually become the norm for the country. The school "was four stories high, with a large auditorium for 700 pupils and twelve classrooms, each of which would accommodate 56 students" (Tyack 1974, 44).

The egg-crate school gave evidence then, as now, that "architectural form" liberates and constrains "educational function" (Tyack 1974, 44). The contemporary version of the large schools is reflected in the modern-day high school being compared to a large shopping mall in which there is something for everyone under one roof or one campus (Powell, Farrar, and Cohen 1985). According to Powell, Farrar, and Cohen, while the shopping mall high school is efficient, its overall effectiveness is suspect.

As the efficiency movement was transforming industry, it was logical for many to infer that the same principles of efficiency could also work their magic in the educational system. It was assumed that what was good for the business world was good for the educational world. While finding resources to fund and staff schools is a chronic issue, efficiency would be the *primus inter pares* — the first among equals — of the different dominant values for this period of time.

Even though there would be different *primus inter pares* as the educational system emerged, the growing reliance on efficiency, again in part because of limited resources, but mostly the embracing of scientific principles for management, would leave an indelible imprint. Subsequent reforms would in part either succeed or fail according to their ability to work with the existing infrastructure of schools (Fuhrman and Lazerson 2005; Tyack and Tobin 1994).

The dominant attractor of efficiency would eventually be challenged as emerging demands on the curriculum required the system to adopt additional purposes. Growing enrollments and scientific advances called for a more diversified and practical curriculum. An informative report from Yale came out in 1828 that reflected the competing philosophies in education and argued for halting the vocationalizing of the curriculum at Yale. The *Yale Report* challenged the basic assumptions of the time regarding the purpose of formal education and who should participate. The report became one of the more influential reports of the time, articulating the issues between the old and new curriculum at the existing colleges (Pak 2008).

The same technological advancements stimulating the Industrial Revolution were challenging the assumptions governing education at this point in time. The traditional education curriculum equipped the elite with a classical education that was designed to develop and hone the students' mental faculties through the study of the ancient languages, pure mathematics, and literature. In addition, the deeply learned man needed to be adept in the art and science of communicating, hence the emphasis on rhetoric, oration, and composition.

The technological innovations required institutions of higher education to become more relevant by discovering new knowledge rather than preserving old knowledge. The encroachment of the natural and practical sciences would soon make the ancient curriculum irrelevant to the new industrial society. At the same time, filling the desks was an influx of students with a broader range of abilities and motivations who, unlike previous generations of students, were not destined for careers in the theological, medical, and legal disciplines. A change in the curriculum from one that only the elite could (and wanted to) master to one that was more inclusive, such as offering the agricultural, mechanical, and vocational arts, would eventually result in different standards of excellence associated with a college education.

The impetus for the *Yale Report* was to "inquire into the expediency of dispensing with the study of the ancient languages, as part of the regular course of instruction" (Committee of the Corporation 1828, 5). The distinguished faculty of Yale crafted a response that articulated what made for a "SUPERIOR EDUCATION" (emphasis in original report, 6). While the report recognized the movement toward establishing an immediate connection between one's education and future profession, it argued that a classical liberal arts education is what ultimately best equips individuals for their eventual profession. By developing the requisite mental powers, comprehensive views, and elements of character, a classical education laid the adequate foundation for any and every profession.

The *Yale Report* was an attempt to broaden a classical education for the growing professions and vocations, not just the elite. The advances in science would now make professional education necessary and feasible for a greater number of students than a classical curriculum historically was able to recruit and retain. As stated in the report,

> It is said that the public now demand, that the doors should be thrown open to all; that education ought to be so modified, and varied, as to adapt to the exigencies of the country, and the prospects of different individuals; that the instruction given to those who are destined to be merchants, or manufacturers, or agriculturalists, should have a special reference to their respective professional pursuits. (24)

The *Yale Report* unequivocally claimed that for the sake of excellence the "college has its appropriate object and they [other institutions for learning] have theirs" (24). It was not that the committee did not think professional schools and other vocational institutions were not warranted; they did not want the vocational curriculum to undermine the distinctive mission of a thorough education at the college level. Opening the doors for additional programs and students threatened to "depress its standard of merit" and inherit students of "inferior aims and attainments" (26). The committee believed that a "thorough education ought therefore to be extended to all classes" (29).

The Yale Committee also recognized that expanding enrollment numbers would threaten academic quality, claiming the "competition was for excellence, rather than for numbers" (27). By opening the doors to more students, and more programs, the committee believed educational standards would be lowered. The *Yale Report* articulated a meritorious set of standards in education that kept the intellectual and moral development at the heart of the curriculum, thereby limiting access to higher education to individuals with certain aptitudes, abilities, and motivation.

The classical curriculum by itself was feasible when there were a limited number of elementary and secondary students to draw from to fill the relatively few roles in society that required deeply informed and eloquent individuals. Now the changes of urbanization and industrialization required a different type of educated individual. While excellence was the nonnegotiable defining the type of secondary and postsecondary education people were receiving, the stage was now set to radically alter and expand the nature of academic excellence from its narrow historical use (e.g., a classical education).

As pressure to expand the purposes for school intensified, a similar clash was emerging regarding the religious nature of the curriculum. Acrimonious and violent showdowns occurred in New York City and Philadelphia in the 1840s, ironically enough, over individual liberties regarding the type of religion allowed in the classroom. Free School societies emerged in cities like New York City and Philadelphia to educate youth who could not otherwise afford school. The Free Schools took on a Protestant version of "non-sectarianism" (Ravitch 2000; Lannie and Diethorn 1968).

As government schools in various states grew in size due to increased immigration and urbanization, educational governance was centralized. While neighborhoods remained relatively homogenous, combining several neighborhoods into one school brought to the surface problematic differences. Designing a nonsectarian curriculum that everyone could agree on proved more difficult than originally assumed.

The early government schools naively claimed to be nonsectarian in their use of the Protestant Bible readings and teachings. The surging Irish-Catholic population in New York City and Philadelphia in the 1820s and 1830s began to overflow into the government schools. A critical mass of Catholic leaders and families now challenged the sectarian version of a "nonsectarian" Protestant education.

On February 25, 1840, the Roman Catholic Church officials in New York City submitted a request for public aid from the state common school fund to subsidize Catholic education. The rationale was that the nonsectarian form of Protestantism was antithetical to Catholic teachings and therefore undermined the faith of Catholic students enrolled in the Free Schools (Ravitch 2000). The basic reasons behind the proposal were articulated in printed exchanges between various Catholic newspapers. One Catholic periodical that spoke for the Church hierarchy,

> held that Catholic schools are an integral part of the state common school system. Their reasoning was that the schools of the Public School Society

were Protestant public schools, while their own schools were "Catholic public schools," equally entitled to public support. Only this system of public support, they believed, could achieve the state's object of universal education "without forcing the professors of any religion to act against their conscience." (as cited in Ravitch 2000, 41)

As to be expected, the Protestants opposed the motion while other sectarian religious groups joined the Catholics in requesting subsidies for their schools so that they could educate their students in a manner consistent with the tenets of their faith. The trustees of the Public School Society adopted a resolution that "if religious instruction is communicated, it is foreign to the intentions of the school system, and should be instantly abandoned. Religious instruction is no part of a common school education." (Document 80, The Committee on Arts and Sciences and Schools, 1840, as cited in Ravitch 2000, 44).

What the society failed to appreciate was that retaining nonsectarian Bible reading from the King James Version of the Bible was in Catholic standards a form of heretical sectarianism. The Catholic Bible contained the Apocrypha (seven additional books in the Old Testament not part of the Protestant Bible) and translated specific passages differently than the King James Bible.

While sensitivities toward the Catholic concerns were developed, after much politicking, derogatory exchanges, and riots, the powers that be decided that Catholic and other sectarian groups would not be eligible for funds for their public schools and the Protestant Bible was retained as a standard part of the curriculum in the New York City government schools. The passionate and articulate crusader for the Catholic school movement in New York was Archbishop John Hughes, who after the controversy "made the establishment of a Catholic school system the first priority of the church" (Ravitch 2000, 80).

Similar exchanges and policy outcomes also took place in Philadelphia, except that in the city of brotherly love, the Philadelphia Bible riots of 1844 took on a more violent component resulting in deaths and the destruction of property. Tensions ebbed and flowed in heated verbal exchanges resulting in armed confrontations in early May and July 1844. As in New York City, the Catholic leadership was arguing under the rubric of individual liberty that what practices were proper for the Protestant student should be afforded to the Catholic student.

While for the most part, the Free School Society of New York City thought retaining the Protestant Bible was nonsectarian, the Protestants in Philadelphia took a more militant and explicit position in promoting Protestantism over the "heretical" Catholicism. The religious wars in Philadelphia were over critical distinctions of revealed truths and the resulting moral implications on students. Neither side would give up without a fight, thinking the stakes were too high for a compromise. While both sides believed that religion was necessary for a good education, the conflict was over whose version of Truth should be taught in the schools.

The Catholic school wars were evidence that religiously neutral education was indeed not neutral. New initial conditions prepared the way for only K–12 government schools to receive state and local funding. The previous practice of the state and local monies being used to subsidize private and religiously affiliated schools consistent with parents' individual liberties was replaced with funding for only nonsectarian schools as a means of keeping the peace with diverse religious beliefs now occupying the classroom. In deference to neutrality, albeit a false deference, the politics of the Catholic school wars resulted in the abandonment of previous voucher programs that would have allowed any student (equality) to receive a subsidized education in the school of his or her choice (liberty).

The stage was now set for government schools to emerge and eventually transform the educational landscape. The seeds of a comprehensive system of nonprivate mass education were germinating. Previous reform policy such as the Massachusetts Laws of 1642 and 1647 gave evidence to the conviction that education was necessary for nation building. The states now went from making education compulsory to making school participation compulsory (Meyer et al. 1979).

Justification for compulsory schooling abounded. Depending upon who was asked, compulsory school laws were implemented to

1. Provide an alternative and meaningful experience to the inhumane child labor laws at the time (Urban and Wagoner 2004),
2. "Americanize" the growing influx of the bored and unsupervised immigrant youth whose idleness promoted delinquency (Tyack 1974),
3. Develop surrogate parents in lieu of the failure of biological parents to provide for the proper development of their children (Gaither 2008), or

4. Create a literate and educated citizenry necessary for the building and
maintaining of a superior and successful republic (Mann 1848).

While it was probably a combination of all four, the justifications resonated with the dearly held beliefs of a relatively young republic such that
a critical tipping point in the system was reached.

While Europe had a dual system of education that favored the aristoc-
racy, Horace Mann, the zealous father of the common school movement,
appealed to America's founding and dearest held principle of equality
when he argued that a universal government school system, beyond all
other institutions, would be the great equalizer in building a superior
republic (Mann 1848). Through the Herculean efforts of Mann, Massachusetts passed the first compulsory school law in 1852, which eventually
cascaded into every contiguous state implementing some form of compulsory schooling by 1918 (*Biennial Survey of Education in the United
States* 1921).

The sectarian school wars and compulsory education laws now required
that every child be in school with the state providing free nonsectarian
education in the government-run schools to those families who could not
afford what was once publically supported private education. State-sup-
ported nonsectarian education (which is an oxymoron—nonsectarian is a
form of sectarianism) was an attempt to provide an educational system that
did not promote one world view at the expense of other world views.

Concurrent with the movement of opening up education for the masses
as a necessary condition to building a more perfect nation was the expansion of enrollment opportunities in the postsecondary environment. An
increase in the number of postsecondary institutions and the expansion
of program offerings was necessary to build a competitive and growing
republic in a changing society. Similar to the provisions in the Northwest
Ordinance Act of 1787 in terms of setting aside land for schools, the Morrill Act of 1862 allowed for states to sell federal lands with the proceeds
used specifically for the establishment of state institutions of higher learning that offered both a liberal and a useful arts curriculum.

As referenced in the *Yale Report* of 1828, the encroachment of a technical curriculum was displacing the more classical curriculum at institutions
of higher education. The scales were officially tipped in favor of the vocational offerings in the useful arts in 1862 with the Morrill College Land

Grant Act. The Land Grant Act funded the establishment of agricultural, mechanical arts, mining, and military science programs at institutions of higher learning for each state. What became known as land-grant institutions, A&M (agriculture and mechanical arts) colleges sprouted up across the country, legitimizing existing colleges of higher learning already devoted to the vocational arts (Thelin 2004).

Justin Smith Morrill initiated his land-grant bill in Congress in 1857 only to have it vetoed by President James Buchanan. Undeterred, Morrill introduced a modified version of the bill to Congress in 1861 to have the bill eventually signed into law by President Abraham Lincoln in July 1862 (Lucas 1994). The driving purpose of the act was to endow, support, and maintain at least one college

> where the leading object shall be, without excluding other scientific and classical studies, and including military tactics, to teach such branches of learning as are related to agriculture and the mechanic arts, in such manner as the legislatures of the States may respectively prescribe, in order to promote the liberal and practical education of the industrial classes in the several pursuits and professions in life. (*Morrill Act* 1862, sec. 4)

In 1890 the second Morrill Act was passed to expand access to higher education by providing additional endowments and prohibiting racial discrimination at existing land-grant institutions. States could elect to create separate land-grant institutions for blacks in the segregated South, which resulted in the founding of seventeen historically black land-grant colleges (National Association of State Universities and Land Grant Colleges 1995).

The Land Grant Acts were designed to meet the growing need for agricultural and mechanical education and "provide a broad segment of the population with a practical education that had direct relevance to their daily lives" (National Association of State Universities and Land Grant Colleges 1995, 3). The principles of excellence and equality generated the need for A&M-like institutions of higher learning. Jischke (2004), speaking at the time as president of Purdue University, stated in a Justin Smith Morrill lecture that the Morrill Act "was a concept for higher education that was deeply rooted in the American democratic ideal that opportunity should be available to everyone and that education was the vehicle for that opportunity" (Jischke 2004).

The American educational system was maturing as an essential institution in building the republic. Compulsory schooling for youth would ensure a literate and informed citizenry necessary to sustain a vibrant democracy. It logically followed that expanding postsecondary educational opportunities would make for a competitive and thriving republic.

The *Yale Report* of 1828 articulated the competing philosophies and respective values of a classical education and vocational education at the college level. The Morrill Land Grant Acts legitimized the practical or applied arts at the college level and made higher education accessible to the industrial class. Compulsory education made elementary education free and, therefore, accessible, albeit mandatory, to the masses but had yet to resolve whether the curriculum should take a more practical perspective. This would come out of necessity at a later date, only after some resistance by those who tenaciously held on to the cherished view that the type of education good for the elite was also necessary for the masses.

As to be expected with compulsory school laws, school enrollment was increasing. This expanding enrollment led to subsequent changes to the curriculum. Kliebard (1995), in his book *The Struggle for the American Curriculum: 1893–1958,* reports that

> one immediate impetus for change came as a consequence of a massive new influx of students into secondary schools beginning around 1890. In 1890, only between six and seven percent of the population of youth fourteen to seventeen years old was attending secondary school. By 1900, it was already over eleven percent, and in 1920, about a third of that age-group was enrolled in secondary schools. (7)

With expanding enrollments, the question regarding what ought to be taught reemerged with one answer generated from the National Educational Association (NEA) Committee of Ten.

The Committee of Ten was appointed by the NEA in July 1892 to report on the optimal high school curriculum or curricula to equip students for college and meet the differing college admission requirements of the existing institutions of higher learning. While the impetus was to standardize the secondary curriculum and university admissions criteria in order to create a more efficient alignment, the design was an attempt to shape an excellent secondary curriculum so that any student, regardless of his or her destination, would have the mental faculties to do well.

Chaired by Charles Eliot, president of Harvard University, the committee consisted of five university presidents (including Eliot), the commissioner of education (William T. Harris), one university professor, and three secondary school principals. Nine subcommittees with ten different participants on each contributed different recommendations for the final report. Forty-seven out of ninety participants were from institutions of higher learning and the remaining from the secondary school environment.

Unsurprisingly, the finished report developed an ambitious high school curriculum. The committee accommodated pseudodiversity and choice within the secondary school environment when it designed four curricular programs (Classical, Latin-Scientific, Modern Languages, and English). Yet the overlap of so many core academic subjects among the four programs and the noticeable absence of vocational courses made it evident that the high school curriculum retained a college preparatory rendition of excellence.

While the committee acknowledged only a small percentage of secondary students would actually go on to college, all would be served well by an "elitist" curriculum. It is a compelling commentary that while the vocational fields were already making inroads at the postsecondary level, as discussed in the *Yale Report* and legitimatized by the Morrill Land Grant Acts, they were ignored by a committee and subcommittee with a majority of representatives from the ivory tower.

The final report from the Committee of Ten in 1893 was reminiscent of the *Yale Report* of 1828. Both reports espoused an ideal curriculum under the rubric of excellence. Unfortunately the reports did not accommodate the realities of the changing society in allowing for different educational outcomes that served the different needs of society at that time. The recommendations from the Committee of Ten failed to be implemented because the "elitist" view of school did not match the practical realities of the expanding student body.

Differentiation of the curriculum, while addressed on the surface by the Committee of Ten, was at the forefront of the next reiteration of reforms, in which the traditional assumptions on the purpose of school were expanded. While the movement of vocationalizing the curriculum was already afoot, forces converged to bring about the Smith-Hughes Act of 1917. The act established in the educational psyche that secondary schools would serve as the pipeline, not only for colleges and universities, but now for a variety of vocations. The act also, for the first time, directed federal funding to the secondary school environment (a precursor of more things to come regarding the federal government's involvement in K–12 education).

The act provided for the

> promotion of vocational education; to provide for cooperation with the States in the promotion of such education in agriculture and the trades and industries; to provide for cooperation with the States in the preparation of teachers of vocational subjects; and to appropriate money and regulate its expenditure. (National Vocational Education (Smith-Hughes) Act 1917)

Home economics, vocational art, and agricultural courses were to become legitimate components of the American curriculum. Kliebard (1999) astutely asserts that "the Smith-Hughes marks the point when vocationalism began to gain ascendancy over rival educational ideals" (132).

Concurrent with the ideas and pragmatics of education leading to the emergence of the Smith-Hughes Act was the work of another NEA committee tasked with articulating a cohesive national policy on the purposes of secondary schools. The needs of society were changing so that the role of schools had to shift in order to take up the slack. Children in an agricultural society were apprenticed in a whole array of subjects in their homes by their parents. The Industrial Revolution and large influx of immigrants required schools to socialize students to appropriate mores and customs of being good Americans and provide an alternative for students who would otherwise occupy the streets.

In one sense, compulsory education was a means to provide for children what parents working in the factories could no longer do at home. As a result, the school was positioned to be a surrogate parent and eventually replace the role of the home in terms of feeding the students (school cafeterias), providing onsite health care (school nurses), and an array of social services along with courses in physical and home economic education (Gaither 2008; Tyack 1974).

In multiple ways, the schools became the alma mater—the kind mother, in lieu of the biological mother. An underlying assumption of public education was that the state knew better than the parent and was in a better position than the parent to provide for and teach students all things necessary.

Seven broader aims than the traditional concepts of school were articulated in the NEA's *Cardinal Principles of Secondary Education* promulgated in 1918. In stark contrast to the NEA's Committee of Ten's four "college-preparatory" tracks, the NEA Committee on the Reorganization of Secondary Schools "sought to match courses of study with the probable destinations or classifications of secondary-school students" (Kliebard 2002, 45). The 1918 committee report called for the reorganization of secondary education citing the changes in society, school populations, and educational theories.

The seven objectives for education, in perceived cumulative order, advocated for were

1. Health
2. Command of fundamental process
3. Worthy home membership
4. Vocation
5. Citizenship
6. Worthy use of leisure
7. Ethical character

Noticeably absent from the list was intellectual development, only hinted at in command of fundamental process, which was proficiency in reading, writing, arithmetic, and oral expression (National Education Association 1918). The committee went on to recommend comprehensive high schools with differentiated curricula that effectively and efficiently socialized and sorted students according to their perceived familial, social-civic, and vocational destinies.

The landmark report marked the transition from schools serving primarily an intellectual function to providing a comprehensive and necessary function in which there was something for everyone. Eventually high schools, while still retaining vestiges of the factory model, would assume a shopping mall metaphor (Powell, Farrar, and Cohen 1985).

The Industrial Revolution had ushered in an "every man for himself" and "survival of the fittest" mentality. The illusion of a meritocracy was perpetuated in the rags-to-riches success stories of people like Andrew Carnegie, J. D. Rockefeller, J. P. Morgan, and Henry Ford. The Industrial Revolution created profound and obvious disparity between the haves and the have-nots. The social condition of the have-nots emerged to eventually preclude many, if not the most, competent of individuals from achieving a level of success. The Industrial Revolution, with all of its positives, exacerbated poverty and exploitation so that some type of social and political response was warranted.

This response was known as progressivism.

Progressivism is the term applied to a variety of responses to the economic and social problems rapid industrialization introduced to America. Progressivism began as a social movement and grew into a political movement. The early progressives rejected Social Darwinism. In other words, they were people who believed that the problems society faced (poverty, violence, greed, racism, class warfare) could best be addressed by providing good education, a safe environment, and an efficient workplace. Progressives lived mainly in the cities, were college educated, and believed that government could be a tool for change. Social reformers, like Jane Addams, and journalists, like Jacob Riis and Ida Tarbel, were powerful voices for progressivism. They concentrated on exposing the evils of corporate greed, combating fear of immigrants, and urging Americans to think hard about what democracy meant. (Eleanor Roosevelt Papers Project 2003, 1)

Progressive idealists and reformers recognized that society and government played a role in equalizing opportunity. Theodore Roosevelt (TR) articulated the essence of his progressive platform in a speech delivered on Labor Day, September 7, 1903, at the New York State Agriculture Association when he persuasively argued that every individual was entitled to "a square deal." The betterment of society and survival of the republic was predicated on individuals receiving a square deal rather than being exploited (Roosevelt 1903).

The square deal mentality resurfaced in the form of a "new deal" thirty years later when Franklin D. Roosevelt (FDR, fifth cousin to TR) rallied government resources to enable society and individuals to succeed in life. Over fifty years earlier Horace Mann explicitly connected progressivism with education in his twelfth annual and final report to the Massachusetts Board of Education, stating that "education then, beyond all other devices of human origin, is a great equalizer of the conditions of men,—the balance wheel of the social machinery" (Mann 1848, as cited in Cremin 1957, 87).

While progressive reformers, politicians, and movements abounded in the late 1800s and early 1900s, a prodigy and articulate spokesman for progressive reform for education emerged. As Mann helped get everyone in school to be taught what was considered necessary at the time, the baton passed to John Dewey to help every student learn what was necessary. Dewey (1900/1902) articulated well the tensions regarding whether school serves society or the student. In the former, society teaches every child the same thing (what every student needs to know to be a good American) in the same manner. In the latter, society allows the child to learn different things differently, according to his or her disposition. The debate was often erroneously framed as an either-or dichotomy when in reality Dewey argued for a balance between both positions with dual emphasis on the individual child in the form of a student-centered and content-driven curriculum in lieu of an emphasis solely on the curriculum.

Dewey advocated active learning (versus passive learning associated with the traditional classroom) in what became known as the student-centered approach in the form of guided experiences. Dewey provided a range of choices in the curriculum by encouraging exploration and self-discovery in the classroom around specific standards. Dewey argued that a student-centered curriculum was more efficient, not in terms of standardized instruction and exams, but that an education that did not engage the students was an education in which students did not learn.

Dewey's philosophy of education resonated with many people, but was unfortunately mischaracterized and translated as diluted of standards, rigor, and cohesive learning (Dewey 1935). In addition, Dewey's emphasis on individualized instruction challenged the growing emphasis on efficiency already imprinted on the system and gaining even greater momentum at the turn of the century. As evident in the Lancaster model of instruction and in the egg-crate design of schools, limited resources dictated efficient ways to teach as many students as possible. Efficiency had so transformed industry such that an automatic and unchecked assumption was that the principles of scientific efficiency should and would effectively transfer to the educational environment.

Dewey's model of education was antithetical to the factory metaphor of education with the standardized curriculum managed by a bell schedule in large egg-crate-like classrooms. Dewey posited that teaching fifteen to twenty students the same thing in a variety of ways at various rates was more effective, and, hence, more efficient than teaching twenty-five or more students in one classroom the same thing the same way at the same rate. Dewey's philosophy would be considered too idealistic to be of any practical value, especially in light of the momentum for efficiency and standards.

Efficiency as the dominant value was reinforced with Frederick Taylor's *Principles of Scientific Management*, published in 1911. As one of the earlier efficiency experts, Taylor's principles were applied to approximately two hundred American businesses between 1901 and 1915, helping him and his ideas gain widespread popularity (Lazonick 2005). What was good for business was believed to be equally good for education, especially at a time when, as stated by Calvin Coolidge in 1925, "After all, the chief business of the American people is business" (Coolidge 1925).

Taylor (1911) persuasively documents that the whole country was experiencing a great loss "through inefficiency in almost all of our daily acts" (70). Taylor reports that the remedy for the everyday "inefficiencies lies in systematic management" (7). Taylor went on to claim that "the fundamental principles of scientific management are applicable to all kinds of human activities" (7). Taylor argued that rules and laws effectively and efficiently streamline processes and "replace the judgment of individual workers" (4). Bureaucracy, policies, and procedures theoretically bring about compliance.

Another educational practice based upon advances in science energizing the efficiency movement was the advent of intelligence testing. In 1905, Alfred Binet developed the first test to measure intelligence. Binet was motivated to identify slow learners in order to target additional learning resources (Lemann 2000). In 1916 Lewis Terman of Stanford University expanded the Binet test to become a measure of innate ability in what was known as the Stanford-Binet IQ test, which "became the most widely used individual mental test for the next two decades" (Ravitch 2001, 134). Schools were administering IQ tests to sort students into "appropriate" unskilled, skilled, and college curriculum tracks to eventually become a "routine feature in American public schools" (Ravitch 2001, 155).

The testing industry expanded with the advent of World War I as a mass number of army recruits were tested to quickly sort potential officers from nonofficer personnel. In addition, the mass number of recruits helped provide an expanded data pool to "norm" a standardized measure of intelligence. The military intelligence test was transformed into the SAT exam and utilized to identify who had the innate ability to do well in college. The SAT was designed to identify the capable students for college study and make college opportunities more accessible to the masses, rather than just the elite (Lemann 2000). Since 1926 the SAT has dominated the college placement scene, theoretically helping students and admission officers from institutions of higher education (IHE) discern a good match between students and respective universities.

Intelligence testing was a harbinger of standardized tests that would eventually become entrenched in the educational system (Sacks 1999). Given the cost and time associated with measuring the complex phenomena of academic achievement, the temptation to acquiesce to a quick measure in the form of a high stakes standardized test was too great. Efficiency became the dominant value over excellence in determining how and what to assess regarding academic achievement, more recently resurfacing with renewed emphasis on standardized testing associated with the No Child Left Behind Act of 2001 (signed by President George W. Bush on January 8, 2002).

Another vestige of the efficient past that continues to constrain innovation and achievement is the Carnegie unit, or standard student credit hour. As high school enrollments expanded from less than 5 percent of the eligible students at the turn of the century to 15 percent by 1910, college theoretically became accessible to more prospective students (Shedd 2003). As a result, some type of metric was needed for colleges to assess which high school programs provided adequate preparation for the rigors of college. Instead of assessing individual students, a default rubric for academic units was implemented.

The NEA's 1894 *Report of the Committee of Ten on the Secondary School Studies* declared that

> every subject which is taught at all in a secondary school should be taught
> in the same way and to the same extent to every pupil. Thus, for all pupils,
> who study Latin, or history, or algebra, for example, the allotment of time

and the method of instruction should be the same. (National Education Association 1894, 17)

Student learning was now inferred by a measurement of time spent in a
course. Time-based academic units allowed for the efficient alignment of
high school courses with college admission requirements. While the credit
hour did not originate with the Carnegie Foundation for the Advancement
of Teaching, the foundation indirectly facilitated its widespread adoption
in 1909 (Shedd 2003). If colleges wanted to accept faculty retirement
allowances from the Carnegie Foundation (established in 1906 with a
$10 million gift from Andrew Carnegie to provide pensions for college
faculty), they needed to implement the "Carnegie unit" as a component
of their admissions requirements (Shedd 2003). "By 1910 almost all high
schools measured course work by the Carnegie unit" (8). As a result, time
spent on learning would be embedded in the system as a means to standardize instructional units and the typical school schedule.

MORE OF THE SAME (FRACTALS),
FEEDBACK, AND HOMEOSTASIS

As the land of opportunity, America emerged such that every person
(equality) could pursue a better life (excellence) as he or she saw fit (liberty) and could afford (efficiency) according to his or her abilities and
motivations. As the educational system was beginning to mature and become more complex, the values or dominant strange attractors competed
and oscillated between each other to be the first among equals. The rate
of reform was bound to accelerate as the educational system became more
complex. Growing enrollments resulted in more schools. The learners and
society were becoming more diverse, resulting in broader purposes and
means of education.

At the turn of the twentieth century, students who were not necessarily
destined or bound for a four-year university education were now graduating from high school with no place to go. The convergence of variables
led to an inevitable and unique American development in the educational
system—the community college movement (Diener 1986; Koos 1925;
Fields 1962). In 1901 the first junior college was formed in Joliet, Illinois.

The community college movement and its "isthmian function" (Koos 1925) was to expand accessibility and equal opportunity for postsecondary education unlike any other educational institution or system. The associate arts degree as preparatory for an advanced degree was legitimatized by William Rainey Harper. In his annual report as the president of the University of Chicago, Harper suggested that the first two years of college work could be completed at some high schools throughout the states, thus making college more accessible (Harper 1901).

Those who received a free government education in the elementary and secondary environment soon realized the same principles of democracy warranted similar provisions at the postsecondary environment. Fields (1962) states,

> The drive to maintain a greater and greater degree of democracy in all of our social arrangements has been a most important influence. The junior college movement was born during the late nineteenth and early twentieth centuries, when democracy and an equal opportunity for all were strongly advocated. The possibility of attending college in the local community served to offer this equal opportunity. (55)

By 1920 the junior college movement earned a place in education when it had its first national meeting and developed a national organization, the American Association of Community Colleges. As junior colleges grew in popularity, they would inherit broader purposes than just preparing students for their junior and senior years of postsecondary study to include a range of vocational training in which an associate arts degree would suffice.

The various vocational and advanced college preparation functions of the two-year college were further legitimized when the 1947 President's Commission on Higher Education recommended that junior colleges be referred to as "community" colleges rather than "junior" colleges in order to reflect the broader and immediate purposes in serving the educational and business needs of local communities (Zook 1948). The commission report acknowledged the vital role community colleges could serve in equalizing educational opportunities by providing "programs for the development of other abilities than those involved in academic aptitude, and they [colleges] cannot continue to concentrate on students with one type of intelligence to the neglect of youth with other talents" (Zook 1948, 32).

The report went on to establish an agenda stating that "it is obvious, then, that free and universal access to education, in terms of the interests, ability, and need of the student, must be a major goal in American education" (36). The report advocated making education equally available to all with tuition-free education up to the fourteenth grade and relatively low tuition for the subsequent years of university study.

The report generated much debate regarding who should participate in college and how and what college students should be taught so that, by 1953, there were over five hundred articles on the commission's report (Hutcheson 2007). The report (in conjunction with returning World War II veterans who needed requisite technical education) was also a catalyst to the biggest growth spurt for community colleges. The number of community colleges had more than doubled by 1971 to 847 colleges from the 328 public community colleges in 1947 (Cohen and Brawer 1989). There are currently 1,132 public community colleges in the United States educating 35 percent of the student college population in the nation (approximately 58 percent in California; *Chronicle of Higher Education* 2009).

The community college provides students easy and equitable access to a variety of opportunities through proximity, low tuition, and open enrollment. Consistent with the democratic principles of liberty and equality, college opportunities are now available for everyone and are no longer an exclusive enterprise, thanks to the growth of community colleges. Rather than be automatically sorted to a vocational or college-bound track as early as sixth grade, as was the custom of many European and Asian educational systems, students in America can self-select their educational trajectory to and through various postsecondary options.

A catalyst to the community college movement and expansion of postsecondary opportunities was the 1944 Serviceman Readjustment Act, more popularly known as the G.I. Bill. Designed to strategically help approximately eight million veterans' reentry into society, the G.I. Bill made available an array of benefits, one of which included the cost of college tuition. As a result, "2.2 million pursued a college education or graduate degree, and 5.6 million attained vocational or on-the-job training" (Mettler 2005, 345).

As college enrollments swelled, the myth that college was only for the few well-to-do was shattered. With the G.I. Bill as the catalyst, college completion rates for individuals ages twenty-five to twenty-nine rose from 5.9 percent in 1940 to 29.6 percent in 2007 (National Center for Education Statistics 2008b). Higher education was now more accessible than ever with funding from the G.I. Bill and growth in the number of institutions of higher learning initiated by the President's Commission on Higher Education.

Concurrent to the initial growth of community colleges from 1901 to 1947 and the promulgation of John Dewey's progressive ideology for schools, several parallel movements promoting educational equality and liberty would also surface. A milder reiteration of the Catholic school wars of the 1840s emerged in 1925, with the resolution favoring the side for personal liberty (what is good for the individual) rather than equality in the form of neutrality (what is good for the group).

Making good on Archbishop Hughes's commitment to establish Catholic schools as an alternative to the anti-Catholic government schools and dedication to educating students consistent with the tenets of their faith, the Roman Catholics established a network of Catholic schools across the growing United States. This network of Catholic schools emerged to become one the largest providers of private education in the United States (National Center of Education Statistics 2009).

In 1922 the citizens of Oregon passed an innocent sounding referendum titled the Compulsory Education Law. The finer print of the law required students to be enrolled in government-only schools. The referendum made it illegal for parents in Oregon to send their children to Catholic and other private schools within the state. The story behind the legislation was that the impetus for the bill was the Ku Klux Klan's attempt to purify Oregon of Catholics (Slawson 2005).

The Society of Sisters of the Holy Names of Jesus and Mary filed an injunction against the Compulsory Education Act on December 22, 1923. "Consolidating the case with a challenge to the act brought by the Hill Military Academy, a private non-religiously affiliated school, the three-judge district court enjoined the Oregon statue on the grounds that it violated the Fourteenth Amendment" (O'Scannlain 2007, 35). The court also stated that "parents possess a natural and inherent right to the nurture, control and tutorship of their offspring that they may be brought up according to the parents' conception of what is right and just, decent and respectable" (Slawson 2005, 117).

"Governor Walter Pierce, who had been elected with Klan support two years earlier, appealed to the Supreme Court" (Slawson 2005, 117). In *Pierce v. Society of Sisters of the Holy Names of Jesus and Mary*, the Supreme Court decided in favor of individual liberty when they declared that

> the Society's bill alleges that the enactment conflicts with the right of parents to choose schools where their children will receive appropriate mental and religious training, the right of the child to influence the parents' choice of a school, the right of schools and teachers therein to engage in a useful business or profession, and is accordingly repugnant to the Constitution and void. (*Pierce v. Society of Sisters* 1925)

The decision also asserted that it was

> entirely plain that the Act of 1922 unreasonably interferes with the liberty of parents and guardians to direct the upbringing and education of children. . . . The fundamental theory of liberty upon which all governments in this Union repose excludes any general power of the State to standardize its children by forcing them to accept instruction from public teachers only. The child is not the mere creature of the State; those who nurture him and direct his destiny have the right, coupled with the high duty, to recognize and prepare him for additional obligations. (*Pierce v. Society of Sisters* 1925)

While compulsory education was a nonnegotiable at this time, utilizing strong rhetoric, the Supreme Court adamantly upheld liberty as the dominant principle when it came to what type of education was required. On June 1, 1925, the Supreme Court legitimized private and religious schools as an alternative to government schools when enforcing compulsory education.

As the Society of Sisters was fighting the status quo to promote academic freedom and diversity, progressive educators were continuing their quest to deviate from the limiting influence of the existing curriculum. The value of a standardized philosophy of K–12 education with narrowly restricted purposes over a system with multiple philosophies and purposes was empirically challenged from 1933 to 1941 in what became known as the Eight-Year Study. The study was sponsored by the Commission

on the Relation of School and College of the Progressive Education Association (PEA; Kridel and Bullough 2007). The goals of the study were
to "establish a relationship between school and college that would permit
and encourage reconstruction in the secondary school" and "find, through
exploration and experimentation, how the high school in the United States
can serve youth more effectively" (Aikin 1942, 116).

The gist of the experiment was that 284 colleges agreed to give 29 high
schools latitude from the traditional high school curriculum (Kridel and
Bullough 2007). Participating schools explored and experimented with
curriculum and school structure while retaining an emphasis on subject
content and participating in standardized testing and various accountability measures.

> During the 1930s, *exploration* and *experimentation* were hallmarks of
> progressive schools as teachers sought ways to continuously improve the
> educational experience for all youth. Commission leaders realized that the
> experiment meant breaking the hold of the Carnegie unit on secondary
> school curricula. If programs of study could be developed embracing the
> tenets of progressive education without sacrificing the academic preparation
> of the college-bound student and other, then the PEA would have greatly
> advanced its case for experimentation. (Kridel and Bullough 2007, 5)

One of the more popular components of the study was the College
Follow-up Study, "which compared the college grade point averages
of 1,475 students who attended participating schools to the averages of
1,475 students who attended an assortment of traditional high schools"
(Kridel and Bullough 2007, 6). While as a whole the experimental group
performed slightly better than the traditional group, the more progressive of the schools "substantially outperformed their peers in terms of
academic averages and honors, intellectual traits, and personal and social
responsibility" (6).

The legacy of the study is explained by Kridel and Bullough (2007):

> The lasting testimony of the Eight-Year Study demonstrates that educators
> can experiment with secondary school practices in ways that lead to greater
> curricular coherence, stronger democratic communities for teachers and
> students, and innovative programs that are responsive to the needs of ado-
> lescents, regardless of their career and education choices. (5–6)

The Eight-Year Study demonstrated that exploring and experimenting with instruction, as long as it was coupled with a serious commitment to substance, was more effective than traditional programs. The advent of World War II would minimize the success stories of progressive education and usher in a return to narrowly defined traditional curriculum. The return would provide a false sense of security to the next war generation, regardless of the fact that school enrollment had expanded at unprecedented rates. High school enrollments had already doubled from 15 percent in 1910 to 32 percent in 1920 (Shedd 2003). High school graduation rates grew from 9 percent in 1910 to 50 percent in 1940 (Goldin and Katz 2008). While schools were attracting a more diverse range of learners, the exigencies of war would pressure the system to default to an efficient one-size-fits-all curriculum.

In the interim, as progressive education was making the American educational system more democratic, extreme versions were emerging only to taint and distort what progressive education initially represented. One such version was the Life Adjustment Movement. In 1945 the U.S. Office of Education convened a conference to discuss vocational education in order to prepare for the anticipated increase in youth unemployment associated with soon to be returning veterans (Ravitch 2001). The chairman of the committee, Charles Prosser, issued the following statement, in what would become known as the Prosser Resolution.

> It is the belief of this conference that . . . the vocational school of a community will be better able to prepare 20 percent of its youth of secondary school age for entrance upon desirable skilled occupations; and that the high school will continue to prepare 20 percent of its students for entrance to college. We do not believe that the remaining 60 percent of our youth of secondary school age will receive the life adjustment training they need and to which they are entitled as American citizens—unless and until the administrators of public education with the assistance of the vocational education leaders formulate a similar program for this group. (Office of Education 1948, 15)

A life adjustment curriculum of nonintellectual subjects and cocurricular activity would serve the largest constituency of the secondary school, and hence redefine the high school experience accordingly. The Prosser Resolution launched a national crusade by the U.S. Office of Education to host regional and national conferences and reshaped the high school curriculum to include courses around "basic" and "social" learning in lieu of participation in many traditional academic requirements (Office of Education 1948; Ravitch 2001). To serve the "remaining 60 percent" of the students in high school, the curriculum needed to be expanded to include trivial-sounding courses instead of the more rigorous vocational and college preparatory curriculum.

Even as early as 1934 the Office of Education documented a phenomenal increase in course offerings in the secondary school that was associated with the increase of secondary school students. The number of courses expanded from approximately 16 subjects in 1895 to more than 206 by 1934 (Office of Education 1938). In addition to an increase in the number of nonintellectual courses, while the enrollment in high school had expanded to slightly over 80 percent in 1955, enrollment in physics, geometry, and foreign language courses had declined to 4.6 percent, 11.4 percent, and 20.6 percent, respectively (National Center for Education Statistics 1993; Ravitch 2001). The high school curriculum expanded to facilitate retention of a more diverse range of students at the expense of a rigorous academic program for even the most capable.

Critics of the "dumbing down of the curriculum" trend in education emerged from various fronts. One of the most notable opponents was Vice-Admiral Hyman Rickover. Rickover, known as the father of the nuclear submarine, earned numerous medals and decorations for his service to the country and was featured in the January 11, 1954, *Time* cover story. Disturbed by the prevalent absence of academic rigor in the educational system, Vice-Admiral Rickover (1959), turned education reformer, lamented that

> in the American comprehensive school the pupil finds a display of courses resembling the variegated dishes in a cafeteria—some useful to everyone (physical training), some useful to college-bound children (mathematics and sciences), some useful to future parents, homemakers, beauticians, printers, fishermen, and what have you. Out of this mass of subjects the child then chooses his fare. No wonder he often gorges himself on sweets instead of taking solid meat that must be chewed. (143)

University history professor Arthur Bestor also bemoaned the life adjustment curriculum and the accompanying unrealistic expectations for schools to be all things to all students. Bestor posited that the diverse curricular and cocurricular offerings undermined the schools' essential purpose of intellectual development (Bestor 1953). In his book *Educational Wastelands: The Retreat from Learning in Our Public Schools,* Bestor states,

> The idea that the school must undertake to meet every need that some other agency is failing to meet, regardless of the suitability of the schoolroom to the task, is a preposterous delusion that in the end can wreck the educational system without in any way contributing to the salvation of society. Much of the cant about education for "home and family living" is a disguised way of saying that the school must take the responsibility for things that the family today is supposedly failing to do. If family life is in a perilous state, that is a national calamity. But it does not mean that we can or should reproduce its intimacies in the school room. . . . The school promises too much on one hand, and too little on the other, when it begins to think so loosely about its functions. (75–76)

As education took on a more inclusive and democratic role in terms of making the curriculum accessible to more students, a foundation was laid for even more consequential changes. The progressive reform agenda surfaced and rectified some of the inequities and deficiencies in the educational system only to, inevitably, raise other latent imbalances of inequality. The progressive agenda of achieving excellence and equity would cascade at an accelerated rate in the 1950s, 1960s, and 1970s.

Brown v. Board of Education (1954) was a unanimous and long-awaited Supreme Court ruling that changed America (Williams 2004; Ravitch 2001). A few brief paragraphs on *Brown* cannot do justice to the complexity and stories leading up to and after the 1954 civil rights landmark decision. The court ruled that "in the field of public education the doctrine of 'separate but equal' [adopted in *Plessy v. Ferguson* (163 U.S. 537)] has no place" (*Brown v. Board of Education* 1954, 495). In essence, the practice of segregation in schools based solely upon race was declared illegal as separate educational facilities were declared "inherently unequal" (495). Citing the Fourteenth Amendment, the court ruled that the plaintiffs in the case were denied equal protection of the laws.

The story in part begins with *Plessy v. Ferguson* (1896), in which "the U.S. Supreme Court ultimately maintained that, as long as equal facilities were provided to citizens, classification of individuals by race was neither a violation of the Fourteenth Amendment's equal protection clause nor inhibitory of the Black community's advancement" (Guthrie and Springer 2004, 8). As a result of the *Plessy* decision, Linda Brown was required to walk one hour and twenty minutes through dangerous parts of Topeka to attend the all-black Monroe Elementary School. Linda made application for admission to the local white elementary school a few blocks from her home and was denied. Ironically, Linda was denied admission to the Charles Sumner Elementary School, named after a Massachusetts U.S. Senator (1851–1874) and avid civil rights activist before, during, and after the Civil War (Guthrie and Springer 2004).

Originally defeated in the U.S. District Court for Kansas, on behalf of Brown, the National Association for the Advancement of Colored People (NAACP) strategically appealed to the Supreme Court with four similar cases in order to demonstrate that segregation was a national issue and not just an isolated situation (Berman 1966). The Brown package advanced to the Supreme Court in the fall of 1951 with Thurgood Marshall as the lead attorney representing the NAACP. The Supreme Court failed to reach a decision by the end of the 1952–1953 term and scheduled rearguments for October 1953 (Berman 1966). Arguments ended on December 9, 1953, leaving over five months for the Court to render and draft its unanimous landmark decision.

School desegregation did not automatically happen after May 17, 1954, when the decision was announced. The Court recognized the inherent and "considerable complexity" associated with implementing the principle of equality across so many unique school settings that an implementation decree warranted more time (*Brown v. Board of Education* 1954, 495). The attorneys general of the states practicing segregation were permitted to appear before the court as *amici curiae* by October 1954 (*Brown v. Board of Education* 1954). In what is known as the Brown II decision, *Brown v. Board of Education*, 1955, the District Courts were to implement desegregation policies "with all deliberate speed" (*Brown v. Board of Education* 1955, 301).

The Court captured the sentiment of the nation regarding the role of education in American society. In the opinion, the Court acknowledged that "education is perhaps the most important function of state and local governments . . . [and] where the state has undertaken to provide it [education], is a right which much must be made available to all on equal terms" (*Brown v. Board of Education* 1954, 493). Unfortunately, the immediate and future civil rights policies and practices did not advance at deliberate speed, but the foundation was strengthened for future milestones toward equality to emerge in the subsequent decades. In the interim, the country would confront new challenges that would divert focus from reform around equality to a refocus on excellence.

A TIPPING POINT AND SELF-ORGANIZED CRITICALITY

The life adjustment movement and the social causes of desegregation resulted in a de-emphasis of the intellectual purposes of school. In the fall of 1957, Americans were frightened into perceiving that the American educational system was lacking academic rigor to the danger and peril of the country. Bestor (1953) and Rickover (1959) had been sounding the alarm that educational standards were falling. Bestor documented how the aims of American education had been intentionally lowered in deference to distorted understandings of progressive education, the practical and social needs of students, and life adjustment training.

While schools were taking on a social agenda and offering various curricular and cocurricular activities, intellectual development became secondary, if not tertiary. The emphasis would temporarily change when the first space satellite appeared over the horizon. On October 4, 1957, the Soviet Union launched Sputnik into space as shocked and already scared Americans imagined what the cold war Soviet power would do now that they were ahead in the rocket and space race.

Soon after Sputnik, the federal government asserted a new role in education that forever positioned and legitimized federal involvement in education. The National Defense Education Act (NDEA), approved September 2, 1958, provided almost a billion dollars' worth of categorical aid to the states for enhanced math, science, language, and vocational educational programs. Section 101 of Title I—General Provisions of NDEA states,

The Congress hereby finds and declares that the security of the Nation requires the fullest development of the mental resources and technical skills of its young men and women. The present emergency demands that additional and more adequate educational opportunities be made available. The defense of this Nation depends upon the mastery of modern techniques developed from complex scientific principles. It depends as well upon the discovery and development of new principles, new techniques, and new knowledge.

We must increase our efforts to identify and educate more of the talent of our Nation. This requires programs that will give assurance that no student of ability will be denied an opportunity for higher education because of financial need; will correct as rapidly as possible the existing imbalances in our educational programs which led to an insufficient proportion of our population educated in science, mathematics, and modern foreign languages and trained in technology. (*National Defense Education Act of 1958*, Title I, Sec. 101)

National security and accompanying cold war rhetoric was the justification used in NDEA and subsequent federal legislation (the Elementary and Secondary Education Act of 1965 was part of Johnson's War on Poverty reforms; *A Nation at Risk,*1983, used the analogy of a cold war to alert Americans to the danger of mediocrity in the American public schools) for the federal government to take a leading role in education.

NDEA acknowledged how close it was to crossing the once very distinct and taboo-like line of no federal involvement in education. Section 101 declares:

The Congress reaffirms the principle and declares that the States and local communities have and must retain control over and primary responsibility for public education. The national interest requires, however, that the Federal Government give assistance to education for programs which are important to our defense.

To meet the present educational emergency requires additional effort at all levels of government. It is therefore the purpose of this Act to provide substantial assistance in various forms to individuals, and to States and their subdivisions, in order to insure trained manpower of sufficient quality and quantity to meet the national defense needs of the United States.

Section 102 of NDEA makes explicit, lest there be any ambiguity from Section 101, that federal government was not taking control of education.

> Nothing contained in this Act shall be construed to authorize any depart-
> ment, agency, officer, or employee of the United States to exercise any
> direction, supervision, or control over the curriculum, program of instruc-
> tion, administration, or personnel of any educational institution or school
> system.

NDEA offered financial resources to the states, institutions of higher
education, and local educational agencies to better resource science, math,
foreign language, and technology programs. NDEA appropriated almost
one billion dollars toward a variety of program initiatives. Low-interest
loans for college students, financial assistance for strengthening science,
math, and foreign language instruction, national defense fellowships, language centers and institutes, media-enhanced instructional materials, and
area vocational education programs were instituted to restore a level of
academic rigor to the educational system.

Seven years later, the next major federal legislation to influence
school curriculum emerged; this time rather than focusing on raising
the academic standards, the emphasis was a return to equality. Lyndon
B. Johnson declared "unconditional war on poverty" in his State of the
Union address on January 8, 1964 (Johnson 1964a). Part of that War on
Poverty included massive legislation on education. As the teacher who
became president, Johnson declared on September 28, 1964, at the two
hundredth anniversary convocation at Brown University, "At the desk
where I sit in Washington, I have learned one great truth: The answer for
all of our national problems, the answer for all the problems of the world,
comes down, when you really analyze it, to one single word—education"
(Johnson 1964b).

President Johnson was joined by his first teacher, Kate Deadrich Loney,
at the dramatic signing of the Elementary and Secondary Education Act
(ESEA) on April 11, 1965, at his former elementary school in Johnson
City, Texas (Halperin 1975). The ESEA provided an initial authorization
of $1.3 billion to be distributed through five categorical programs, primar-
ily providing resources for the classrooms of areas with high concentra-
tions of low-income families (Eidenberg and Morey 1969).

McGuinn (2006) demonstrates that with ESEA "an important thresh-
old had been crossed and an important federal role in education policy
cemented" (33) and a "crucial beachhead to those who sought to further

increase the federal role in education policy" (37) had been established. ESEA positioned the federal government to take an active role in education beyond the historical and passive role of compiling statistics, eventually to snowball or emerge in the twenty-first century as a primary player in shaping educational policies and practices. McGuinn documents how federal spending on education grew from 8 percent to 16 percent from 1960 to 1985 (37) and additional amendments and reauthorizations expanded such that "by 1980 the Department of Education administered approximately 500 different Federal Education programs" (39).

The Department of Education was initially established in 1867 by an act of Congress. The primary function was to gather statistics on the condition of education and disseminate useful information to promote education throughout the country. Two years later the department was reassigned to the Department of the Interior for the next seventy years and functioned as an Office of Education, retaining its original functions. In 1939 the Office of Education was relocated in the new Federal Security Agency, which in 1953 became the Department of Health, Education and Welfare. In 1979, the office went through a substantive upgrade in status when an autonomous cabinet-level Department of Education was created, further legitimizing and positioning the federal government to take a more active role in the American classroom (Sniegoski 1988).

Senator John Williams of Delaware prophetically announced greater intrusive federal involvement in education, albeit not anticipating a separate cabinet-level Department of Education, on the day the Senate approved ESEA:

> This bill, which is a sham on its face, is merely the beginning. It contains within it the seeds of the first Federal education system which will be nurtured by its supporters in the years to come long after the current excuse of aiding the poverty stricken is forgotten. The tragedy of this legislation is that it plays on the honest desire of people across the country to assist the needy, now that the approaches used through the years have been thoroughly discredited. The needy are being used as a wedge to open the floodgates, and you may be absolutely certain that the flood of Federal control is ready to sweep the land. (Senator Williams, *Congressional Record*, April 9, 1965, S7710)

Representative Howard Smith expressed similar concerns when he lamented,

> We apparently have come to the end of the road so far as local control over education in public facilities is concerned. I abhor that. There is nothing dearer to the American home than the neighborhood school, where you have your PTA and your different organizations, and all take a vital role in the school and have control of it. I hate to see that tradition destroyed and control removed from the little neighborhood in the country and located in the bureaucracy of Washington, but I think I see the handwriting on the wall. This is the day that the bureaucrats in the Education Department have looked forward to and have fought for a good many years. (Representative Smith, *Congressional Record*, March 24, 1965, H5729)

Senator Wayne Morse readily acknowledged at the time that ESEA was a legitimate victory that allowed for federal involvement in elementary and secondary schools "through the back door" (Senator Morse, *Congressional Record*, April 7, 1965, S7317). Congressman John Rhodes stated that the bill "advertised as an attack upon the problems of educationally deprived children, is, instead, an assault upon State and local control of education" (Representative Rhode, *Congressional Record*, March 24, 1965, H5766).

Subsequent reauthorizations of ESEA generated additional programs and federal legislation in the immediate and long-term future (with the latest reiteration found in the No Child Left Behind Act of 2001, signed into law January 8, 2002). ESEA spawned the Education for All Handicapped Children Act of 1975 that stipulated that if states wanted to receive federal funding they must develop and implement policies that assure a free appropriate public education to all children with disabilities. McGuinn (2006) astutely documents that

> a 1966 amendment to ESEA created a new title (Title VI) to provide grants for programs for "handicapped" children. This new program—like ESEA itself—continued to expand over time as the definition of "handicapped" was broadened to cover more and more students. In 1970, for example, Title VI was broken off from ESEA and expanded to form a separate Education of the Handicapped Act. This later became the Education for All Handicapped Children Act (1975) and, in 1997, the Individuals with Disabilities

Education Act (IDEA). Despite a decline in the total public school population between 1968 and 1986, the number of children in special education programs in the United States during that period increased from 2.3 million to 4.3 million. Special education programs became the fastest-growing part of the state and local education budget and the second-largest federal education program. (38)

Prior to the 1960s, children with special needs attended segregated institutions that were perceived better suited to meet their unique needs. As *Brown v. Board of Education* revealed, separate systems typically meant inferior and unequal learning environments (Osgood 2005). Momentum for special education students to be fully included in traditional classrooms to whatever extent possible was now legally mandated in 1975 with the passage of All Handicapped Children Act (AHCA). AHCA was reauthorized in 1990 as the Individuals with Disabilities Education Act (IDEA) and again in 1997 with additions that stressed individualized instruction in the least restrictive environment (Osgood 2005).

Equity legislation cascaded into additional equality-based reform initiatives. The Bilingual Education Act, added as Title VII to ESEA in 1968, provided symbolic and financial resources for programs to support students whose inability to speak English put them at an educational disadvantage (Crawford 1991). The Civil Rights Act of 1964 protected individuals from discrimination in public facilities and education. The Economic Opportunity Act of 1964 was responsible for the emergence of the Head Start program that was initially housed in the newly created Office of Economic Opportunity. Head Start was created to better prepare children in poverty for school by providing early education, health, and social services to eligible families.

The Higher Education Act of 1965 (HEA) was to higher education what ESEA was to elementary and secondary education in terms of making education more accessible. HEA was intended "to strengthen the educational resources of our colleges and universities and to provide financial assistance for students in postsecondary and higher education" (*Higher Education Act of 1965*, intro.). HEA was amended in 1972 to include the landmark Title IX provision, which provided that "No person in the United States shall on the basis of sex, be denied the benefits of, or be subjected to discrimination under any education program or activity receiving Federal financial assistance" (Title IX 1972).

Equal educational and school athletic opportunities for women created opportunities for women to excel and expand their participation rates such that

> from 1970 to 2006, women's undergraduate enrollment increased over three times as fast as men's, surpassing men's enrollment in 1978. In this period, women's enrollment rose from 3.2 to 8.7 million (an increase of 178 percent), while men's rose from 4.3 to 6.5 million (an increase of 53 percent). From 2007 to 2017, both men's and women's undergraduate enrollments are projected to increase, with women maintaining 57 percent of total enrollment. (Planty et al. 2008, 9)

Title VI and VII of ESEA, EOA of 1964 and subsequent Head Start programs, and HEA and Title IX of HEA Amendment Act of 1972 made education accessible to what were otherwise excluded or marginalized groups, eventually generating additional legislation that expanded both the letter and spirit of the original laws, and enlarged the role and spending of the federal government in education. Brimley and Garfield (2005) document that "in 1960, the federal funds for education were $1.7 billion; in 1980, $25.6 billion; in 1993, $30.6 billion; and in 2003, $63.2 billion in the Education Department's budget" (212).

Educational standards were being displaced once again as schools were becoming all things to all people to accommodate the diversity of students' aptitudes, abilities, and interests. In 1983, the lack of emphasis on academic rigor and standards resulted in one of the "most comprehensive, most referenced, and most controversial study on excellence in U.S. education" (National Commission on Excellence in Education 1984, book cover) from the relatively new cabinet-level Department of Education. The wave of reform in the equity era (1954–1982) solidified the mind-set that education was an automatic right more than a meritorious privilege.

A National Commission on Excellence in Education was called by Secretary of Education T. H. Bell in August 1981 to assess the quality of education in America and identify appropriate recommendations. In April 1983 the commission issued their report, titled *A Nation at Risk: The Imperative for Educational Reform*. The introduction poignantly declares,

> Our Nation is at risk. Our once unchallenged preeminence in commerce, industry, science, and technological innovation is being overtaken by

competitors throughout the world. This report is concerned with only one of the many causes and dimensions of the problem, but it is the one that undergirds American prosperity, security, and civility. We report to the American people that while we can take justifiable pride in what our schools and colleges have historically accomplished and contributed to the United States and the well-being of its people, the educational foundations of our society are presently being eroded by a rising tide of mediocrity that threatens our very future as a Nation and a people. What was unimaginable a generation ago has begun to occur—others are matching and surpassing our educational attainments.

If an unfriendly foreign power had attempted to impose on America the mediocre educational performance that exists today, we might well have viewed it as an act of war. As it stands, we have allowed this to happen to ourselves. We have even squandered the gains in student achievement made in the wake of the Sputnik challenge. Moreover, we have dismantled essential support systems which helped make those gains possible. We have, in effect, been committing an act of unthinking, unilateral educational disarmament.

Our society and its educational institutions seem to have lost sight of the basic purposes of schooling, and of the high expectations and disciplined effort needed to attain them. This report, the result of 18 months of study, seeks to generate reform of our educational system in fundamental ways and to renew the Nation's commitment to schools and colleges of high quality throughout the length and breadth of our land.

That we have compromised this commitment is, upon reflection, hardly surprising, given the multitude of often conflicting demands we have placed on our Nation's schools and colleges. They are routinely called on to provide solutions to personal, social, and political problems that the home and other institutions either will not or cannot resolve. We must understand that these demands on our schools and colleges often exact an educational cost as well as a financial one.

On the occasion of the Commission's first meeting, President Reagan noted the central importance of education in American life when he said: "Certainly there are few areas of American life as important to our society, to our people, and to our families as our schools and colleges." This report, therefore, is as much an open letter to the American people as it is a report to the Secretary of Education. We are confident that the American people, properly informed, will do what is right for their children and for the generations to come. (National Commission on Excellence in Education 1984, 5–6)

The "rising tide of mediocrity" and cold war language highlighted in the report was a reiteration of the call for uniform standards and academic excellence in schools articulated in the 1950s reform associated with Sputnik and the National Defense Education Act of 1958. As a result of *A Nation at Risk,* state governments began to take a more deliberate role to address issues of quality, temporarily ending the equity regime at the heart of ESEA and ushering in a zeal for accountability in education (McGuinn 2006; Sacks 1999).

Governors met in the fall of 1989 to establish an ambitious agenda to develop national goals for education. In the fall of 1991, President George H. W. Bush announced his America 2000 education reform plan that emphasized educational outcomes. Previous federal legislation emphasized funding for programs, whereas America 2000 and subsequent federal legislation focused on results around specific achievement goals (McGuinn 2006). America 2000 was the precursor to President Clinton's Goals 2000 legislation that provided incentives for the states to develop standards-based reforms. The 1994 reauthorization of ESEA, titled Goals 2000: Educate America Act, targeted eight ambitious goals that focused on outputs rather than inputs associated with previous federal legislation. States were now required to implement school improvement plans and content standards to accomplish the itemized goals.

As the federal government was taking a larger role in shaping American curriculum, the dominant value of choice was beginning to resurface with new momentum and noticeable impact on the educational system. In contrast to federal and state policy dictating what was included and excluded in the school curriculum, a subset of parents still preferred the option to pursue an educational system that best aligned with their values and goals for their individual children. Under the banner of individual liberty and choice, the Milwaukee Parental Choice Voucher Program emerged in 1990 and the first Charter School law was passed in Minnesota in 1991.

Voucher plans provide for the partial or full cost of students' education in the form of a voucher that parents use to purchase education in either a private or public school of their choice. There are privately and publically funded voucher programs. The logic behind publically funded voucher programs is that the fixed amount that state and local governments spend for each student to receive a free education should be converted to a voucher that allows parents to compete for available slots at schools of their choice, including private school options. Publically funded vouchers go directly to the parents, who in turn submit the vouchers to the school of their choice. An emerging version of vouchers is tuition tax-credit programs. In a few states, parents spending money on private school tuition are eligible for a corresponding state tax credit.

Voucher programs were first encouraged by Adam Smith in 1776 as a means to support both the public and private interests associated with formal education. Public funding of parent-run schools would ensure the democracy had an educated citizenry. Local-parental control of schools would allow formal schooling to be an extension of the family by sharing similar values and outcomes.

A century earlier, as the common school movement was progressing, Americans like Horace Mann looked to Prussia for a model. The United States' model of common and compulsory education borrowed heavily from the Prussian system of education that provided subsidies to private and religious enterprise to establish and maintain schools (Jones 1918). In a *Report on the State of Public Instruction in Prussia,* Cousin (1835) documented that at its zenith, Prussia welcomed and embraced the help of private enterprise (i.e., the churches and synagogues) to establish national goals in a manner consistent with the individual religious traditions. The clergy were assigned duties to oversee schools in their parishes and report student progress to regional authorities.

In addition to historical precedent, the Nobel laureate economist Milton Friedman (1955) advanced a compelling argument for school vouchers that provided the "intellectual foundation for vouchers" (Schneider, Teske, and Marschall 2000, 24) by appealing to the power of the market to create competitive schools in contrast to the current monopoly of government schools.

The arguments for vouchers have expanded to include returning control to parents when it comes to deciding the most appropriate educational experience for their students. In addition to transferring knowledge, schools overtly and covertly socialize students toward particular values and beliefs (Brint 2006). Some of the norms in government schools are in direct conflict with many parents' core beliefs, values, and expectations, typically those associated with religious traditions. Since education is compulsory, the debate continues that parents should have some choice and flexibility in deciding the essential features of their children's educational experience.

State-sponsored voucher programs have experienced a slow growth, in part because school funding and control are highly political and controversial issues. Kafer (2009) documents that "as of 2008, eligible students in seven states, (FL, GA, ME, OH, UT, VT, WI) can receive state-funded scholarships to attend schools that best meet their needs. In four states (IA, IL, LA, MN), parents can take tax deductions or credits for independent school tuition" (9). The public schools' response to vouchers has been the gradual acceptance of charter programs. Charter schools are publically funded and governed institutions that have been granted latitude to offer specialized programs without the bureaucratic constraints found in traditional government schools. Viteritti (2001) writes,

> Charter schools would become the most revolutionary idea in education for the 1990s, a concrete alternative to the factory model of schooling inherited from the nineteenth century. . . . The underlying premise of the charter school was to provide more independence to school-level professionals in exchange for a higher level of accountability. (64)

Charter schools can have distinctive features that attract a certain subset of families. The range of possible types of charter schools is a function of what the market will bear. Charter schools can specialize in math and science, fine arts, language arts, character education, technology, or other legitimate options while others have been designed to cater to specific communities (homeschoolers and various ethnic groups; Harvard Law Review Association 2009). From the 1992 opening of the first charter school in St. Paul, Minnesota, there are now over five thousand charter schools in the United States (Center for Education Reform 2009).

Lips (2008) documents that

> a growing number of American students are benefiting from school choice policies. Twenty years ago, few states and communities offered parents the opportunity to choose their children's school. Today, millions of American students are benefiting from policies that enable parental choice in education.
>
> This year, 13 states and the District of Columbia are supporting private school choice. Approximately 150,000 children are using publicly funded scholarships to attend private school. Millions more are benefiting from other choice options ranging from charter schools and public school choice to homeschooling and virtual education. Still, an estimated 74 percent of students remain in government-assigned public schools. (1)

Along with the growth in charter schools and voucher programs, there has been growing participation in private schools and homeschooling. The National Center for Education Statistics (2008a) documents an estimated 1.5 million students were homeschooled in the spring of 2007. In addition, "the increase in the homeschooling rate (from 1.7 percent in 1999 to 2.2 percent in 2003 to 2.9 percent in 2007) represents a 74 percent relative increase over an 8-year period and a 36 percent relative increase since 2003" (2).

Gaither (2008) documented that changes in the social mores and the 1962 and 1963 Supreme Court decisions outlawing organized school prayers and school-sponsored Bible readings accelerated the growth in religious private education. According to Gaither, "Evolution, sex education, the somewhat vague but powerful notion of 'secular humanism,' and other factors drove many families away from public education" (108). The number of schools affiliated with the Association of Christian Schools International expanded from 1,900 in 1983 to 3,957 in 2005 with a corresponding 176.5 percent increase in student enrollment.

The U.S. Department of Education (2008) reiterated the vital role nonpublic education has in the nation's K–12 educational system.

> Parents have a fundamental right to guide the upbringing of their children, and government has an obligation to respect that right. The nonpublic school community in the United States provides parents with important options for the education of their children. Faith-based and nonsectarian private schools, along with a growing number of children who are homeschooled, account for approximately 13 percent of the school-age population in grades K–12.
>
> The first schools in the U.S. were private schools and currently account for about 24 percent of all elementary and secondary schools, 11 percent of all students and 12 percent of all full-time teachers. Seventy-six percent of private schools have a religious affiliation, while the remaining 24 percent are nonsectarian. A defining characteristic of private schools is choice as families may freely choose private education and private schools generally have the freedom to choose which students to enroll. Private schools vary widely, though their governance structures and enrollment choices are similar features that all private schools share. (1)

While charter schools, voucher programs, and homeschooling remain controversial, they have been gaining momentum as legitimate alternatives to traditional government-run schools. Choice programs are reiterations of previous practices (fractals) advocated by Smith (1776) and the public sectarian schools in America's early history of formal education. Voucher programs and charter schools are not only legitimate options, but as presented in chapter 3, most likely the next wave of reform in the swinging pendulum's path.

The return to vouchers is actually a promising solution to equally accommodate the four dominant values driving educational practices. Educational vouchers provide equal opportunities (equality) for parents to pursue the best (excellence) and most affordable (efficiency) educational opportunities consistent with their respective values and specific inclinations of their children (liberty). Many private schools, especially various Catholic and Christian academies, are able to provide a better quality education at a fraction of the cost of the neighboring government school (Betts and Loveless 2005).

MORE FRACTALS AND SELF-ORGANIZED CRITICALITY

The latest reform at the forefront driving educational practices is the No Child Left Behind Act of 2001 (NCLB), which was the reauthorization of ESEA. Upon his inauguration in January 2001, President George W. Bush made educational reform his top priority. The first bill he sent to Congress was the No Child Left Behind Act. After one year of garnering strong bipartisan support, President Bush signed on January 8, 2002, an act "to close the achievement gap with accountability, flexibility, and choice, so that no child is left behind" (*No Child Left Behind Act* 2002, intro.).

McGuinn (2006) documents that

> the passage of No Child Left Behind in 2002 fundamentally changed the ends and means of federal education policy from those put forward in the original ESEA legislation and, in so doing, created a new policy regime. The old federal education policy regime, created in 1965, was based on a policy paradigm that saw the central purpose of school reform as promoting equity and access for disadvantaged students, a policymaking arrangement that focused on procedural mandates, and a political alignment in which Republicans opposed federal activism and liberals sought to maintain the federal focus on resources and poor and minority students. . . . The policy

paradigm at the heart of the NCLB regime is centered on the much broader goal of improving education for all students and seeks to do so by signifi-cantly reducing federal influence over process and inputs while replacing it with increased accountability for school performance. (193–94)

At the heart of NCLB were mandates to the states to implement annual testing in reading and mathematics in grades 3–8; test students in science at least once in elementary, middle, and high school; demonstrate stu-dents' adequate yearly progress (AYP) leading to 100 percent proficiency in reading and mathematics by 2014; and hire only "highly qualified" teachers (McGuinn 2006). The intended consequence of NCLB was to create incentives and systems for all students to succeed. An unintended consequence was the constricting of the curriculum and educational prac-tices to achieve AYP at the expense of other important curricular and cocurricular outcomes.

The creation of a "high-stakes testing" environment undermined the more essential aspects of teaching and education and, inadvertently, undervalued learning (Nichols and Berliner 2008a; Nichols and Berliner 2008b). In addition, schools would face substantive consequences if they failed to have at least 95 percent of their students take the annual test or make AYP, variables strongly correlated with social economic status and, therefore, out of the school's control (Haas et al. 2005).

NCLB appealed to both equality and excellence, evident by the act's ti-tle, but defaulted to efficiency by limiting measuring AYP to standardized tests in math and English. It is difficult, yet doable, to measure many of the tangible and intangible outcomes of school. While it is more effective, messier, and more complex to have multiple measures of different student outcomes, it is not as efficient as reducing education to one high stakes measurement. Unfortunately, by default, efficiency became the domi-nant value of NCLB, distorting the original intent of improving schools. Schools are now so focused on generating test scores in math, science, and language arts that other critical aspects of the curriculum are marginalized (Nichols and Berliner 2008a; McKim 2007; Cawelti 2006).

Not only has the curriculum been artificially constricted to fit what can easily be assessed, the teaching pipeline has been inadvertently sabo-taged (Malone 2002; Spradlin and Prendergast 2006; Wakefield 2007). First, many experienced teachers are suffering a growing disenchantment with the profession as they are scripted what to teach in order to prepare students for a high-stakes test (Parsons and Harrington 2009; Cawelti 2006; Spradlin and Prendergast 2006). There is little latitude to deal with individual students or other important curricular goals lest teachers deviate from the scripted curriculum. Second, as a result of NCLB, Hill and Barth (2004) note that "teacher retention, while a historical issue, is now a problem of increasing magnitude" (173).

SUMMARY AND CONCLUSION

Thirty-three major reforms have been reviewed for their cumulative and synergistic effects on the evolution (emergence) of the American educational system. The reforms that emerged appealed to one or more dominant values (strange attractors). The later reforms were reiterations (fractals) of early reforms and transpired when they did as corrections to the swinging pendulum (cybernetics and change) in order to keep the system in equilibrium (homeostasis). Some changes had disproportionate effects on the system (sensitive dependence) because of timing and the larger context of specific reforms (self-organized criticality).

The design and implementation of NCLB is the latest of many examples from the past that reveals education's highly complex environment makes it difficult, if not impossible, to find a solution that solves all of the issues at once. As the number of demands on the system and the amount and speed of feedback expanded, the educational system became more complex over time (much like other complex phenomena), such that the system is on the verge of chaos at any point in time.

To complicate matters, the educational system is subject to budget fluctuations. Given limited resources of time, personnel, and money, educational practices will, in part, be constrained by what and who is available to implement quality programs equally. For example, class size is proportional to available resources. In times of recession, as in 2009, elementary classroom sizes exceed thirty and more students in contrast to twenty students or less in previous years. Lean budget years force efficiency to the forefront of the policy patterns.

Just as budgets are related to policies of efficiency, so is technology. Computer-mediated communication and instruction and virtual classrooms and communities potentially provide less expensive and equally as effective alternatives to costly traditional classroom settings. The newest round of technology allows more to be done with less and is proving to be a powerful tool to engage student learning. While the merit of virtual learning communities over traditional settings remains contested, the point is that technology is positioned to minimize some of the restraints in education associated with efficiency.

Educational policy patterns have emerged over time consistent with the rules of complex systems. For the most part, educational policies are reiterations of previous policies and practices driven by the dominate values that ultimately keep the system in relative homeostasis. Each of the educational practices identified in this chapter appeals to the dominant values legitimized in America's founding documents and practices. When the system gets out of sync, self-corrections are made in the form of other policies in order to keep the system in equilibrium.

As documented, some educational policies have had disproportionate impact on the system, in part because of timing, which makes the system both stable and temperamental. The essence of the system remains intact or stable (providing equal opportunity to a range of excellent educational outcomes as efficiently as possible) while the form adopts to new shapes (e.g., changes in the local, state, and federal control of education; expanding accessibility from the elite to the general masses of people regardless of ethnicity and special needs). The shape changes depending on how equality, excellence, choice, and efficiency are manifested and on what takes precedence when.

The concept of self-organized criticality recognizes that some changes have a greater impact on the system than others because of timing. Every now and then, complex systems reorganize to better manage the complexity associated with the system while keeping the dominant values in play. The current educational system is at risk of becoming overwhelmed in accommodating the range and amount of diversity, equally and efficiently, at accelerated rates. Complex adaptive systems on the verge of chaos either give way to total disorder or go through some type of transformation in the form of bifurcation—developing parallel systems.

The following chapter groups the different reforms according to the dominant values in contrast to the quasi-chronological presentation in this chapter. Chapter 3 illustrates the dynamic pattern of policy reforms that are revealed when presented from a nonlinear perspective consistent with the features of complex adaptive systems.

Chapter Three

Leveraging Complexity
at the Policy Level

The more things change, the more they remain the same.

—French proverb

So, there is nothing new under the sun.

—Ecclesiastes 1:9

Those who cannot remember the past are condemned to repeat it.

—George Santayana

Unfortunately, we are doomed to repeat history, not because we are forgetful, but because, consistent with explanations from nonlinear dynamics, the values and patterns that generated history facilitate similar reiterations in the future. While the scale of previous educational reforms will vary in future manifestations, similar reforms will, nonetheless, appear. The metavalues at work in the past that caused certain events to emerge are the same values at work in the present.

This chapter illustrates that history, for the most part, cannot help but repeat itself as present and future events mirror the past. At the same time, the present and future can be mediated, so that, while similarities to the past will exist, improvement can take place when the laws governing nonlinear systems are appropriately leveraged to bring about desired change.

As demonstrated in chapter 1, there is a common architecture behind all nonlinear systems. All dynamic systems play by the same rules. Complexity science explains the rules that govern the metastory and equips leaders

73

and policymakers with the conceptual framework to strategically leverage the hidden rules of how nature works to bring about optimal results.

As outlined in chapter 2, educational policy provides a useful template with which to understand policy patterns through the lens of complexity science. Educational policy, like other policies, originates and reiterates itself over time to keep the particular system in relative stability, consistent with the respective dominant values. This chapter provides a nonlinear presentation of the thirty-three different reforms in the form of graphs to illustrate the hidden architecture governing educational policy patterns. As with chapter 2, while the foil of analysis is education in America, policymakers can apply the principles of complex systems to any public policy arena in any country. For example, Reich (2009) documents how "the pendulum of public trust has swung back and forth between business and government for more than a century. Confidence in one drops, leading to the other to take prominence—until prominence leads to excesses that erode confidence and push the pendulum back" (94).

At another level, political and business leaders would do well to understand the nature of educational reform. Education as a whole (K–12 and higher education) is America's "largest industry" (Brimley and Garfield 2005, 4) consuming proportionately more dollars of state and local general fund budgets than other services and approximately 5.9 percent of the gross domestic product (GDP)—compared to the military consuming 4.7 percent of the GDP in 2007 (Brimley and Garfield 2005; Government Spending in the United States of America 2010).

The societal importance of schooling is evident by the proportion of time children spend in the classroom, the amount of money modern societies invest in education, and the number of people working in schools (Brint 2006). For example, "Schoolteachers are by far the largest occupation classified as professional by the U.S. Bureau of the Census, numbering more than 5.5 million in 2002" (3). Education is rightly such a big investment that policymakers need to get it right.

One final reason, if not the most urgent, that education is used as the unit of analysis is the belief that all policymakers need to understand the history and future of education because the stakes are too high not to. Whether it should be the case or not, Lyndon Johnson's War on Poverty expressed what many people believed at the time, and now take for granted, as an unstated (and unrealistic) assumption that education will solve all our nation's problems. Brint (2006) documents how "today, schooling is often thought to be an all-purpose panacea. More and better education is seen as the best solution to the common problems that ail most societies" (5).

Education does extremely well, given all it has to deal with. The savior complex of education may explain why there are dynamic problems as the system is asked to do too much (feed, counsel, baby sit, educate, and entertain a captive audience with unique and diverse developmental and physical needs). Just as economic departments will not solve poverty, political science departments eliminate war, medical schools cure all diseases, nor business schools eradicate unethical business practices, education alone will not solve our nation's problems. While education cannot be the savior to a nation's problems, it does play a companion role with the family, community, places of worship, and the government in developing human, social, and physical capital consistent with the tenets of the highest ideals.

These misplaced unrealistic expectations upon formal education are also evident by the intense contest over how students should be taught what, when, and by whom. Too many people with different ideas on how to "get it right" have a vested interest in education. As a result, the educational enterprise is very much a dynamic system that is vulnerable to multiple misunderstandings and misplaced hopes.

THE POLICY PENDULUM

The latest educational reform is often naively characterized as the newest fad in a series of fads. Such mind-sets are revealed when seasoned teachers claim that "theories of education come in and out of fashion like the seasons" and "they are tired of being beaten by the pendulum." The relative frequency in which educational fads are accepted and replaced erroneously suggests that the American educational system is whimsical, lacks consistency and coherence, and is at the mercy of the latest trendsetters. Kliebard (2002) astutely posits,

The term *pendulum swing* has become the most widely used characterization of this phenomenon, implying, of course, that educational reform is nothing but a series of backward and forward movements with, in the end, everything remaining in place. Whatever the merits of *pendulum swing* as the controlling metaphor for the course of educational reform, it reflects a profound disillusionment with the enterprise. (1)

Such limited explanations are consistent with the traditional, rational, and linear models of framing change in what are, in essence, complex and dynamic systems. Unfortunately, such perspectives distort the true nature of reform, limit the ability to anticipate or forecast reform, and often sabotage reform efforts before they have a chance to accomplish their intended effect.

Complexity theory explains, in a new way, how individual reforms are actually the retelling of the same old story in educational policy. Complexity theory legitimizes reforms as reiterations or patterns of dominant values in American education and offers insights on how to maximize reforms. The French proverb "the more things change, the more they remain the same" explains why reform in public education is cyclical, continuously sought, and why external parties play such a critical role. The French proverb reveals the essence of how dynamic complicated systems behave. It suggests that reform initiatives are self-correcting measures that maintain the system in a relative state of equilibrium.

When education policy and practices take off too much in one direction, another reform will come along to bring it back to the center; and when that reform takes policy and practice off center, another reform will bring it back to center. Similar to a thermostat, when a social policy fluctuates in any direction at the expense of other social priorities, reform triggers appropriate adjustments or corrections to the system for the desired equilibrium.

As documented in chapter 2, the homeostasis of the educational system appears to hover around four basic and often competing beliefs and values (or strange attractors) consistent with a democratic society (Marshall, Mitchell, and Wirt 1989; Cusick 1992; Stout, Tallerico, and Scribner 1994). The values of *excellence, equality, choice,* and *efficiency* serve as the strange attractors to keep the system in a constant state of change to maintain stability among competing values. Continuous reform around the "metavalues" maintains a relative homeostasis that allows a public school system to effectively educate the masses while accommodating the diverse values and beliefs surrounding education.

The commitment to *excellence* is typically viewed as the attainment of an agreed upon standard that is somehow superior to other levels of attainment. Excellence encourages and promotes individuals to strive for a superior level of achievement. Implied (but often ignored) in the rhetoric of excellence are the concepts of elitism and haughtiness. By definition, excellence is above average achievement. If the level of achievement is something all can do, what differentiates excellent achievement from average or satisfactory achievement?

In addition, an unintended consequence in the rhetoric of excellence is an arrogant focus on a few standards at the expense of multiple possible targets or standards. How does one decide which standards should dominate over others? Another unfortunate unintended consequence of excellence is that the focus is often reduced to performance on a single measure in the form of a high stakes test in lieu of more effective means of multiple and comprehensive assessments.

The commitment to *equality* is the accessibility to opportunities without partiality. It is the guiding belief that everyone should have the same access to educational opportunities regardless of ethnicity, gender, religion, aptitude, and abilities. Equality has opened many doors of opportunity that were previously unavailable to the historically disenfranchised. The unintended consequence of equality is associating equal opportunity with identical abilities. Equality potentially undermines a meritocracy by promoting advancement that does not emphasize achievement.

The commitment to *choice* in private or public school options and curricular programs accommodates diversity of interests and motivations and recognizes individual rights and freedoms. Some families want religious instruction as part of the curriculum and, therefore, select school options accordingly. Not all students are college bound and, therefore, should have the option of certain types of curricular offerings consistent with their personal and vocational interests. Choice accommodates the ranges of student interests, motivation, aptitude, and abilities found in any student body. An unintended consequence of choice is that some will choose unwisely.

The commitment to *efficiency* is the result of limited resources. The basic principles of economy of scales and diminished returns suggest that there are optimal conditions to preserve precious human and financial resources. Efficiency streamlines activities to essential components. At the same time, efficiency can interfere with effectiveness. Parents expect efficient busing schedules, but not at the expense of safety. High stakes testing is one measure of student achievement, but not necessarily the best measure or indicant of a student's attainment. Unfortunately, when efficiency becomes the means to measure excellence in education in the form of standardized tests, education becomes reduced to only what is measured. When the classroom is reduced to scripted lessons in order to prepare students for a test, efficiency has trumped effectiveness.

Americans prize each value with unequal vigor at any given point in time. The values by nature compete with one another to be the *primus inter pares*—first among equals. Excellence can run counter to choice when people define standards differently, hence, undermining the value of a single national or state standard. With choice, people are free to pursue whatever set of standards of excellence they deem appropriate. Excellence is countered by efficiency when schools cannot afford to recruit an army of the best teachers or provide a plethora of curricular and cocurricular offerings for every student. Excellence is counter to equality in that, by definition, some will get left behind, because, as undemocratic as it sounds, not everyone can perform at above average levels on the same measure. The debate over which value should be the prime directive, or first among equals, is what makes educational reform and policies dynamic and continuously up for review.

The following series of figures illustrate how various reform movements fall on a grid of the four competing values to suggest reform is more than an isolated fad, but rather the product of a larger dynamic pattern. As evidenced in the following figures, trends, or patterns of education reform, emerge within the parameters of the strange attractors. The patterns also anticipate what type of reforms will probably emerge in the near future. The authors acknowledge a degree of arbitrariness in selecting which reforms were included and how such reforms were placed on the grid. Other people may place additional reforms on the grid and existing reforms in slightly different locations on the following figures. The placement of each reform on the graph is based upon the stated primary and secondary values of the particular reform relative to other reforms.

Figure 3.1 illustrates how the strange attractors in the form of four non-negotiable values define the parameters of the system. Educational policy reforms will appeal to one or more of the dominant values of excellence,

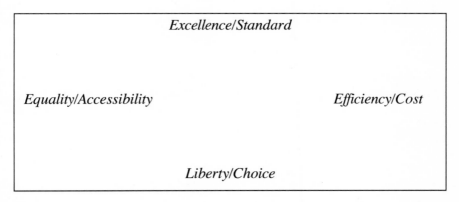

Figure 3.1.

equality, liberty, and efficiency. The reforms in figure 3.2 illustrate the emphasis on excellence, choice, and efficiency early in the system's history, with a preponderance of the reforms defaulting to efficiency as the first among equals.

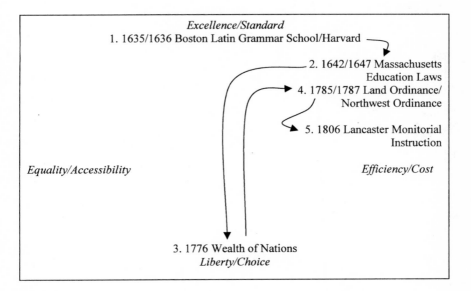

Figure 3.2.

1. **1635/1636.** An early commitment to excellence and the role of education in building a new nation was evident in the creation of the first formal schools.

2. **1642/1647.** Education was deemed necessary in building an excellent nation evident by the earliest recorded education laws. The laws recognized the value of economy of scales by requiring cities of certain sizes to provide corresponding levels of education.

3. **1776.** Adam Smith persuasively argued that public education was best offered as a private enterprise subsidized by the government, appealing to the power of liberty to promote excellent schools.

4. **1785/1787.** As the country expanded, schools were encouraged to promote education and religion by setting aside parcels of land.

5. **1806.** Efficient instructional practices were initiated to educate the masses of displaced youth, keeping the cost of education affordable.

Figure 3.3 illustrates the continued emphasis on excellence, choice, and efficiency.

6. **1828.** The *Yale Report* was a clarion call to retain a high level of excellence at the center of education.

7. **1840–1843.** The Catholic school wars reinforced parents' liberty in choosing the type of educational experience their students received. In ad-

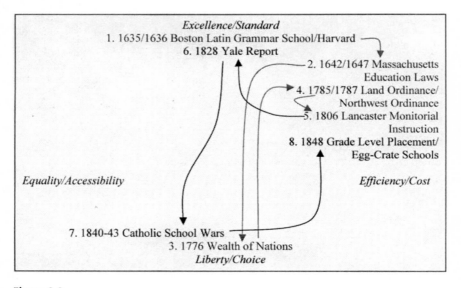

Figure 3.3.

dition, the Catholics demanded to be treated equally in terms of receiving the same funding levels for their schools as their Protestant counterparts were getting.

8. **1848.** Grade placement, bell schedule, and school buildings were created in order to educate students as efficiently as possible.

While early reforms oscillated between excellence, efficiency, and choice, efficiency was the first among equals driving the system at this point in time. As the school system expanded, the infrastructures that mirrored the efficient factory model of productivity (bell schedule, grade placement, and egg-crate-like schools) left its imprint on the system, even to this day some 150 years later. It is logical that new institutions with limited resources default to efficient means to accomplish specific ends. It remains problematic, though, when the infrastructure does change to align with corresponding reforms. As evident from chapter 2 and what follows, as the system matured, the strong imprint of efficiency would limit the impact of additional reforms.

As illustrated in figure 3.4, the next three reforms focused on expanding educational opportunities.

9. **1852.** The first compulsory schooling law in 1852 positioned education to be the great equalizer while developing human capital to sustain a growing nation.

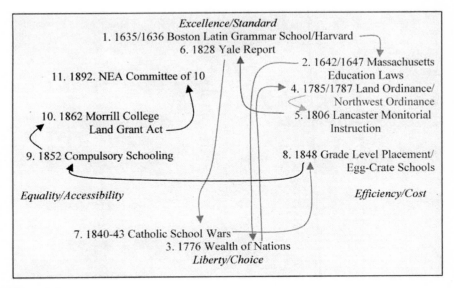

Figure 3.4.

10. **1862.** The Morrill College Land Act ushered in the practical sciences, making college useful for a different set of students and the needs of an industrial society (contrary to the sentiment of the *Yale Report*).

11. **1892.** As enrollment grew, the NEA Committee of Ten acknowledged that schools needed to expand their purposes to be more inclusive and adjust to the changing student demographics, yet retain a classical college preparatory curriculum.

As illustrated in figure 3.5, the next five reforms would cause the pendulum to oscillate around the nonnegotiable values of efficiency, equality, and choice. The regime of efficiency would dominant the direction of the pendulum of reform once again.

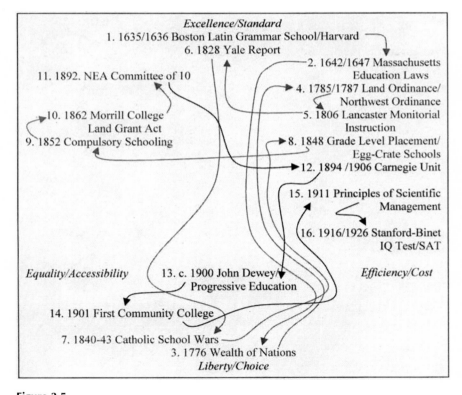

Figure 3.5.

12. **1894/1906.** The NEA Committee of Ten recommended measuring academic units based upon the amount of instructional time in the classroom for each subject versus minimum levels of demonstrated mastery. The standard academic unit soon became known as the Carnegie unit. Similar to the factory work schedule, productivity was measured in units of time, making education all the more efficient. Curriculum was now paced according to what could be taught in the specific time frame with academic grades measuring the level of proficiency students attained in the prescribed window of time. Historically, students advanced once a level of mastery was achieved, regardless of how much time it took to achieve the measurable level of proficiency. Such practices were considered inefficient.

13. **c. 1900.** Concerned about the growing trend toward standardization of an irrelevant and nonengaging curriculum for a growing percentage of students, Dewey launched the progressive education movement. Dewey's message resonated with the emerging need to structure the curriculum around the student and the needs of society. A student-centered and content-driven curriculum would make for an equitable system (something for everyone in a student-centered approach), while retaining standards (content-driven). At the same time, students could gravitate or choose areas of study consistent with their dispositions.

14. **1901.** As a more diverse range of students were graduating from high school who were not necessarily destined or ready for the rigors of university study, alternative opportunities became necessary. The solution was the advent of the community college movement when the first community college opened in Joliet, Illinois, in 1901. College, at least the first two years, was now accessible to a larger portion of students who would not have otherwise had the options to pursue higher education.

15. **1911.** Lest the system get too individualized and therefore cost prohibitive, efficiency-orientated reforms continued to appear. Frederick Taylor's popular treatise on scientific management set the bar for how institutions of society, including schools, should operate. Principles of efficiency were the gospel for systematic management processes. The blueprint for schools was now officially the factory model.

16. **1916/1926.** It was not a surprise that the subsequent reforms of efficiently sorting students by the newly developed empirical-based IQ test and SAT were embraced.

Lest efficiency constrain education too much, additional reforms emerged to maintain equilibrium. The next series of reforms illustrated in figure 3.6 facilitated the educational system to broaden its purposes and hence make education more equitable and empower students with a range of choices.

17. **1917.** The Smith-Hughes Act legitimized diversifying the high school curriculum to include vocational arts, again to accommodate the different types of students now populating high schools and provide the industrial-prepared workers businesses wanted from high school alumni.

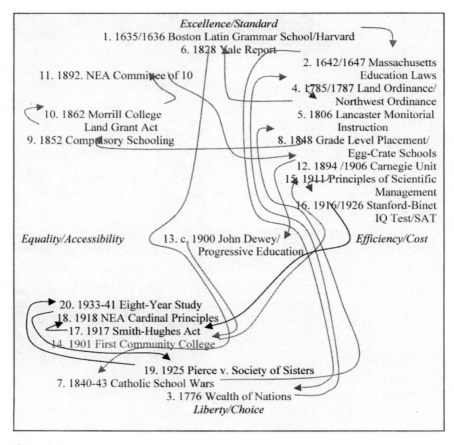

Figure 3.6.

18. **1918.** The NEA Cardinal Principles rectified the short-sightedness of the NEA Committee of Ten Report. The Cardinal Principles expanded the purposes of school to be much more comprehensive and inclusive.

19. **1925.** While schools were becoming more equitable, the Supreme Court case of *Pierce v. Society of Sisters* legitimized parental liberty and choice when selecting schools.

20. **1933–1941.** Consistent with the theme of liberty and equity, the Eight-Year Study demonstrated that schools that implemented a diverse curriculum promoted choice and excellence at the same time.

Evident from figure 3.7, the reform pendulum has shifted from an emphasis on efficiency/excellence-orientated reforms to those focused more on equality and choice. The educational system reached a level of maturity with established infrastructures to process students. The system was experiencing inevitable growing pains taking on broader and more comprehensive purposes. As the system became more inclusive, the stage was set for a cascading of additional equity-based reforms.

21. **1944.** Veterans returning home from World War II needed educational opportunities to make a successful transition to civilian life. The G.I. Bill made higher education available to a mass of adults who would not have normally participated. Just as K–12 education was a perceived right as the great equalizer, the momentum from the increased college participation rates established in the American psyche that higher education was a similar right.

22. **1945.** The Prosser Resolution acknowledged that since schools were educating masses of students, multiple paths and destinations were needed to accommodate the diverse range of aptitudes, abilities, and motivations represented in the classroom. Since 60 percent of the students were reportedly destined to nonprofessional and nontechnical vocations, the curriculum needed to be expanded accordingly.

23. **1947.** The Truman Commission Report strengthened the role of community colleges as necessary institutions to make higher education more equitable, consistent with the founding principle of the nation.

24. **1954.** While issues of equality were being addressed, enough momentum was established to address more grievous and glaring inequities. *Brown v. Board of Education* declared segregation inequitable, and therefore, illegal.

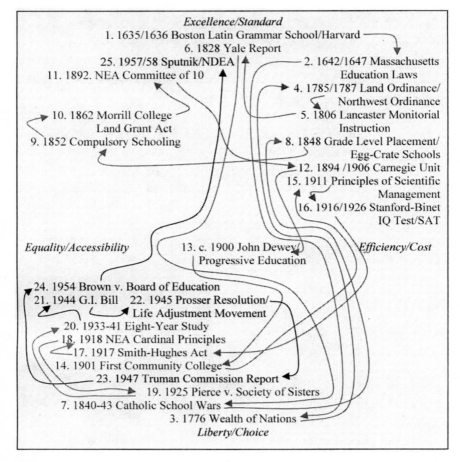

Excellence/Standard
1. 1635/1636 Boston Latin Grammar School/Harvard
6. 1828 Yale Report
25. 1957/58 Sputnik/NDEA
11. 1892. NEA Committee of 10
2. 1642/1647 Massachusetts
Education Laws
4. 1785/1787 Land Ordinance/
Northwest Ordinance
10. 1862 Morrill College
Land Grant Act
5. 1806 Lancaster Monitorial
Instruction
9. 1852 Compulsory Schooling
8. 1848 Grade Level Placement/
Egg-Crate Schools
12. 1894 /1906 Carnegie Unit
15. 1911 Principles of Scientific
Management
16. 1916/1926 Stanford-Binet
IQ Test/SAT
Equality/Accessibility
13. c. 1900 John Dewey/
Progressive Education
Efficiency/Cost
24. 1954 Brown v. Board of Education
21. 1944 G.I. Bill   22. 1945 Prosser Resolution/
Life Adjustment Movement
20. 1933-41 Eight-Year Study
18. 1918 NEA Cardinal Principles
17. 1917 Smith-Hughes Act
14. 1901 First Community College
23. 1947 Truman Commission Report
19. 1925 Pierce v. Society of Sisters
7. 1840-43 Catholic School Wars
3. 1776 Wealth of Nations
Liberty/Choice

Figure 3.7.

25. **1957/1958.** Sputnik and the National Defense Education Act. The equity regime was temporarily interrupted by the launch of Sputnik. The de-emphasis on intellectual development associated with the previous reforms alerted the country in the context of the cold war that academic standards needed to be higher, especially in math and science. NDEA provided resources for the system to promote science and math education.

Figure 3.8 depicts the last eight major educational reforms and illustrates the transition from an emphasis on equity to a regime of policy dominated by standards and accountability.

26. **1965.** The Elementary and Secondary Education Act (ESEA) specifically targeted students needing additional services to succeed in school. The act argued that additional categorical programs were necessary to make schools equitable.

27. **1968.** The Bilingual Education Act specifically targeted students needing additional services to succeed in school, and that without such programs, the curriculum was considered inequitable.

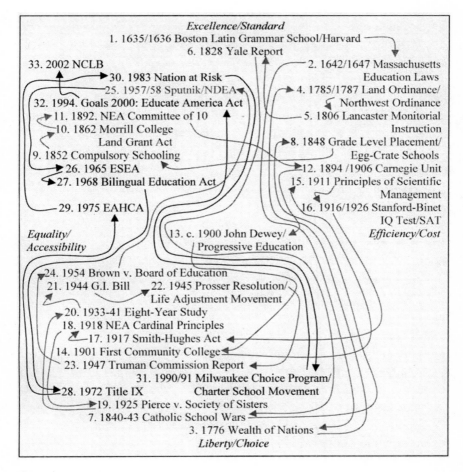

Figure 3.8.

28. **1972.** Inequities associated with gender were addressed with the Title IX Amendment.

29. **1975.** Inequities associated with special needs children were addressed with the Education of All Handicapped Children Act (EAHCA).

30. **1983.** The emphasis on issues associated with equality left the "nation at risk" with a lack of emphasis on academic standards.

31. **1990/1991.** The first publically supported voucher program was launched in Milwaukee in 1990 and the first state law authorizing charter schools was passed in Minnesota in 1991.

32. **1994.** Goals 2000: Educate America Act focused on states implementing academic standards and program improvement plans that emphasized educational outcomes.

33. **2002.** NCLB focused on every student performing at a high level as he or she progressed through the educational system.

Not captured in the preceding graphs are the fluctuating funding patterns and technology advances that influence educational policy. Figure 3.9 illustrates that lean budget years force efficiency to be the dominant value shaping educational practices. Relatively recent advances in Internet technology were the genesis for virtual high schools and online college degree programs, making education accessible and affordable, appealing to both equality and efficiency.

While it is too early to anticipate if Internet technology and resources will be a tipping point that transforms education, Cuban (2003), citing the failure of movies, radio, television, and computers to transform education, documents that when it comes to education, technology has been oversold and underutilized. With the timing of the extreme budget crises of 2009 and the new ways of connecting knowledge with the learner, the system may well self-organize, resulting in a complete transformation of the educational system. At the same time, the behemoth infrastructure may provide enough inertia for any tipping point that disrupts the status quo. Complex systems are relatively stable and temperamental at the same time.

Evident from figures 3.1 to 3.9, a swinging pendulum is inevitable and better than a static pendulum. For example, equality of opportunities evident in the 1960s with various legislation attending to social issues such as the Elementary and Secondary Education Act in 1965, Bilingual

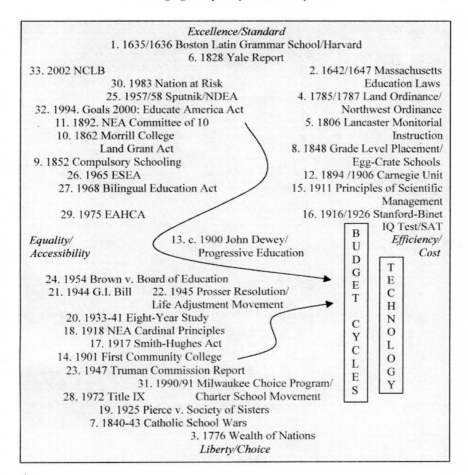

Figure 3.9.

Education Act of 1968 (eliminated with NCLB), followed later by the Education of all Handicapped Children Act of 1975, minimized practices designed to promote excellence.

The promotion of excellence, prompted by Sputnik in 1957 with the National Defense Education Act of 1958, *A Nation at Risk* (1983), Goals 2000, and No Child Left Behind legislation, mitigated the unintended effects of equality being the dominant value in education. The call for equality keeps in check excellence as the only standard that, if left unchecked, would create primarily elitist schools that exclude the masses.

Yet without standards, schools would default to an anything goes type of curriculum.

Whenever there are limited resources, efficiency and cost-effectiveness constrain the system. Efficiency keeps the system from bankruptcy by streamlining policies and eliminating unnecessary programs. At the same time, efficiency can sabotage sound educational practices. The egg-crate school with its group instruction and age-based advancement replaced the one-room schoolhouse with its corollary individualized instruction and achievement-based advancement, in order to efficiently teach more students.

The value of choice provides as many opportunities as possible for divergent constituents. The issue of choice as a dominant value is evident in the legitimization of private educational options in the *Pierce v. Society of Sisters* 1925 case, breadth of course offerings through electives, vocationalizing of the curriculum with the Smith-Hughes Act of 1917, multiple institutions of higher learning including community colleges, vouchers advocated by Milton Friedman beginning in 1955, the first voucher program in Milwaukee in 1990, and the first legislation for charter schools in 1991.

According to Cusick (1992), "Schools are never sufficiently individualized, equal, excellent, or efficient. So education's reform mill never lacks grist" (179). Each value seems to compete with the others in such a way that the overall system maintains a sense of equilibrium. Continuous reform is needed to keep the dynamic system in balance. As more things change (reform), the more they stay the same (appropriate tension among the expression of the four values).

What makes the American system unique is not the competition for dominant values, but rather what dominant values emerged. As explained in chapter 2, one only has to go to the Declaration of Independence and the Constitution to discover how freedom in the form of choice and equal opportunity for all became dominant values in American culture. Excellence emerged as a dominant value as our country became a haven for those who wanted better lives in the context of their individual freedoms. Efficiency is ubiquitous as people are constantly constrained by limited resources from doing everything with the best of everything.

Consistent with complexity theory, educators can and should expect feedback. Education is so critical and value-laden that there are unlimited groups with vested interests in the nature and outcome of education providing essential feedback. Every individual and social group has a vested interest in answering the following questions.

Who should go to school?
What should be the purposes of schooling?
What should children be taught?
Who should decide issues of school direction and policy?
Who should pay for schools? (Stout, Tallerico, and Scribner 1994, 5)

As a result, attempts to influence education are made from a variety of zealous interested parties; hence, feedback is never lacking. Cusick (1992) points out that "our education system includes all sorts of people who want something and who think education, usually someone else's, is the way to get it" (126). There are too many people and groups with a vested interest in the outcome of education to keep silent. Thus, there will be constant competition to align educational needs and values according to the particular values and interests of diverse groups, who in a democratic society have been allowed a voice.

As a pluralistic society, differences in the core values abound. This keeps the debate on reform spirited and ongoing. As long as there are challengers and guardians to the system, which is encouraged in a democratic society, feedback or reform will always be part of the system. Reform is continuous in American education because democracy encourages divergent values and beliefs to have a forum.

If current educational policies are interpreted as compensating for the unintended consequences of previous policies, it is reasonable to infer that future policies will correct for the impending deficiencies in the current reform. The system is working to maintain equilibrium and, therefore, self-corrects over time. Relatively recently, compared to the life cycle of reform (inception, creation, implementation, deterioration), when reform was in the upper left quadrant (see figure 3.8) emphasizing excellence, the system self-corrected toward the equality and choice quadrants of the graph. From 1955 to 1982 there was a concentration of reforms addressing equality and accessibility.

It will not be surprising that the next correction from the extreme emphasis placed upon excellence and standards found in NCLB will gravitate to the "choice" end of the lower left quadrant. The harbinger of that possibility is evident in the recent activities and growth in the charter and voucher programs and the fact that equality and accessibility may have reached saturation. At the same time, as illustrated in figures 3.1–3.9, efficiency policies manifest themselves at various times with renewed vigor and change the trajectory of the existing pattern. The system is especially sensitive to economic fluctuations and technological innovations.

Even though the system is working to maintain homeostasis, it is a dynamic system that is still emerging based upon the initial conditions of the country. New initial conditions continuously emerge to keep the system sensitively dependent on precedent, such that any one reform can potentially serve as a tipping point. As documented in chapter 2, the ESEA proved to be the slippery slope for greater federal involvement in education. With ESEA, federal responsibility in education emerged from a noticeably absent role in the Constitution, to a cabinet-level position, and to major legislation in the form of NCLB that has transformed what happens in the classroom. NCLB's extreme emphasis on high stakes testing inadvertently marginalized other critical aspects of schooling so that a strong compensatory reform is inevitable.

As the system continues to emerge, self-organized criticality suggests the system could bifurcate at any time, especially given the layers of complexity and burgeoning demands placed on the educational system. It is threatening to many that the educational system may become something different than what it looks like today. Change is a good thing, even though it can initially be disturbing and disruptive. The system experienced a major metamorphosis when the common school and compulsory education movement transformed education in America from a free sectarian and locally controlled school system to state-controlled secular government schools. It seems probable and appropriate that the next transformation would be in the direction of vouchers that include locally controlled sectarian nongovernmental schools concurrent with the current government schools. Another probable transformation may be virtual schools, given how technology and instant access to knowledge is transforming the learning paradigm.

SUMMARY AND CONCLUSION

The above argues that continuous reform is a necessary and inevitable component of the educational system. A swinging pendulum is better than a static pendulum. The stakes are too high for anything less. Continuous reform is necessary in maintaining a proper equilibrium between existing values of excellence, equality, efficiency, and choice. Homeostasis between the competing values is maintained to ensure the survivability of the American educational system.

Given the high stakes in educational outcomes, external parties will sustain the pendulum of reform momentum. External parties (e.g., business, government, civil rights groups, politicians, and parents) are necessary for educational reform and provide critical feedback essential for complex systems to prosper. Reform is continuous in American education because democracy encourages divergent values and beliefs to have a forum. Zealous factions and parties with strong vested interests are allowed to influence the who, what, how, when, and why of education. Thanks to technology, the amount and rate of feedback promises to accelerate the rate of reform.

Complexity theory provides a frame of reference to normalize and anticipate reform as reiterations of dominant values associated with a democracy. Educators are encouraged to treat specific reforms as solutions to the underlying tensions of a democracy and integrate the essential message behind each reform, tailoring the reforms to their specific context. In addition, educators are encouraged to judiciously receive the feedback from "reformers" as a valuable tool to maintain an appropriate balance in school policy.

In terms of predictions regarding the future of American public education, complexity theory suggests at least two inevitable outcomes. The trends suggest that choice will play a major role in the next wave of reforms. The direction of reform appears headed to somewhere in the lower left quadrant depicted in figure 3.8. The last two times reform was in the upper left quadrant (1957/1958 and 1983), the reform pendulum swung down to the equality and liberty quadrants. The accelerated growth of charter schools, magnet schools, private schools, and voucher programs

suggests choice is gaining momentum and may be the next wave of reform. The reforms on equality appear to have peaked in the 1960s and
1970s, suggesting also that the next wave of reform will favor the choice
end of the lower left quadrant.

As the educational policy becomes more complex, a major transformation appears likely. The mounting discontent with NCLB, the accompanying angst with high stakes testing, and the burgeoning growth and demands of the system suggest some form of metamorphosis will emerge. In
addition, the amount of feedback and reforms associated with educational
policy seems to have accelerated such that the system is on the verge of
being overwhelmed, if not already.

With so much diversity needing accommodation in the educational
system, the amount of feedback may overwhelm the system to the point
of chaos and eventual metamorphosis. The nation should not be surprised
by, and should even prepare for, an eventual bifurcation. The likely and
legitimate direction of the bifurcation may well be in the form of large-
scale voucher programs. Voucher programs efficiently allow parents an
equal opportunity to choose an education they desire for their students that
is consistent with their values and definitions of excellence.

Regardless of where the system ends up, the pattern reveals an acceptable and legitimate list of alternatives within a range of possibilities,
consistent with the dominant values. The science of complex systems
equips policymakers to treat reform and politics as ongoing contests for
values. Like all contests, victory is relatively short-lived. Policies have
a relatively short shelf life, given that the American society cares about
so many things at the same time. Such recognition may temper extreme
policies (such as NCLB) so as to minimize the number and impact of the
unintended consequences of any one policy that undermine the intended
consequences of any one policy.

Complexity theory helps normalize the swinging pendulum of reform
policy. Change is welcomed as attempted solutions to keep the whole
system in equilibrium. Policy misunderstandings surface because some
people fail to understand the bigger picture. Understanding the nature of
the swinging pendulum equips leaders to better temper the extreme oscil-
lations of the pendulum by attending to the competing values equally in
subsequent reforms.

Complexity theory allows policymakers to anticipate future reforms. While not able to predict the future with precision, a reasonable range of alternatives can be anticipated. Above all, a complexity lens legitimizes the competing values in the system and their respective reiterations. One value should not be ignored at the expense of the others, even though at different times, specific values become the first among equals in terms of defining specific policy.

Chapter 4 provides specific and insightful principles, examples, and illustrations on how to specifically lead complex, nonlinear dynamic systems at both the organizational and policy level.

Chapter Four

Leveraging Complexity at the Organizational Level

Chance favors the prepared mind.

—Louis Pasteur

The first thing that strikes one as characteristic of contemporary leadership is the necessity for the leader to work with and through extremely complex organizations and institutions.

—John Gardner (1990, 81)

Based upon his study of over fifty leaders with exemplary records, Martin (2007) found that great leaders "don't mind a messy problem. In fact, they welcome complexity, because that's where the best answers come from" (66). Martin found that successful leaders honed their abilities to be integrative thinkers who "consider multidirectional and nonlinear relationships among variables" (65). The ability to deal with ambiguity and complexity not only determines how successful a leader will be, it is one of the key factors that determine whether an individual advances in his or her career (Boleman and Deal 2003; Ruderman and Ohlott 1994).

Unfortunately, there are no guarantees in life, only probabilities. Understanding how nature works gives the prepared leader greater odds for successfully navigating the complexity and chaos associated with leadership. As demonstrated in the previous chapters, there are prevalent patterns at work in nature that leaders can leverage to their advantage. Choosing correctly between the many possible dynamic and concurrent patterns in both the macro and micro levels of organizations and policy environments requires wisdom. Complexity science has provided a model in which to recognize such patterns and identify leverage points to manage those patterns of nature. This chapter will take the organizing principles at work in complex systems and develop specific guidelines and practices for leaders to effortlessly sail through the chaos in the organizational and policy environments.

Sailing is an appropriate metaphor for leadership in any complex environment. Seasoned captains make it look easy as they defy natural laws to harness the wind to their advantage. The tacking back and forth and continuous trimming of the sails and rudder allow the captain to sail smoothly into the wind on choppy waters. The strange attractors of the wind, condition of the ship, and desired designation allow the captain to maintain a steady course (homeostasis). The captain is continuously, and ever so subtly, trimming the sails and rudder (changing) to keep an even keel (homeostasis) in response to the compass or dead reckoning (feedback).

At the same time, once under sail, the captain's trajectory continuously emerges as a result of prevailing winds and other environmental demands such as oncoming ships and natural boundaries. Sailors recognize that a small overcorrection with the rudder or an unanticipated gust or shift in the wind can have a big effect in causing the ship to capsize (sensitive dependence on initial conditions). In addition, for a ship to sail smoothly, even in windy and chaotic conditions, the crew needs to follow the lead of the captain, mirroring his or her actions relative to the position of the sail boom (fractals). Seasoned sailors also recognize that a combination of variables at any point in time can have consequential effects such as attempts to avoid an obstacle and a sudden gust causing the sail boom to swing quickly in the opposite direction (a jibe) into unsuspecting passengers (self-organized criticality).

Seasoned leaders, like seasoned sailors, make their efforts look easy and take advantage of the prevailing forces to achieve the desired outcomes. Such leadership requires an intimacy with how dynamic systems work. This final chapter offers practical principles for leaders to sail smoothly in both the micro and macro levels.

The goal of this chapter is to hone, all the more, the leader's ability to skillfully navigate complexity by providing explicit principles and detailed examples to guide one's leadership practices. In the Biblical account, when Solomon recommended splitting a baby in half in order to discern the biological mother of the child, he recognized that the immediate knowledge of the truth to the baby's identity was elusive. Solomon appealed to the metarule that a natural mother would put her suffering beneath that of her own child and, hence, the truth as to the actual mother's identity was easily inferred. Such intimacy with the metarules that govern all nonlinear systems equips leaders to transcend a transactional linear orientation in executing leadership to a transcendent orientation that is characterized as insightful and wise.

The previous three chapters explain and illustrate how dynamic social systems behave in messy yet relatively predictable patterns. The nature of reality is deceptively simple, while appearing complex and even chaotic at times. This complexity is understandable and expected, given that social and physical systems are dynamic—continuously initiating and responding to and within a temperamental environment. The seven simple rules that govern how systems behave are now generalized into the form of principles for executing wise and strategic leadership. The reader should be able to observe similar dynamics from the examples and illustrations provided at work in their own scenarios and utilize the same principles in their leadership practices.

Before moving forward, a disclaimer is offered. What follows are not formulas to guide every leadership decision or planning meeting. What follows may even at times sound contradictory and paradoxical. Every situation is unique and a function of timing (what is going on when). At the same time, there are universal principles at work that can guide leaders in specific situations. Leaders do better operating with comprehensive heuristics than applying the same policy procedures to every situation. Leaders live in ambiguous situations where exceptions are common. Therefore, leadership is very much about making appropriate judgment calls sensitive to the nuances of each scenario.

Complex systems do not lend themselves to precise management formulas and, while systems are to be managed, rarely are they controlled. Guidelines for successful leadership in complex environments, at best, are contingent upon a plethora of variables. It is the rare scenario in which "either-or" (the black and white fallacy) type thinking works. The following guidelines will show that decision making is fluid and deals with a range of "both-and" possibilities. Deciding when to emphasize one nonnegotiable over another, or when to listen to some feedback and ignore other feedback, or when to respond or not to respond to particular changes is a judgment call. The ultimate answer to the question "How do you know what is the right thing to do" is "It all depends." As a result, the following applications of the key concepts are relatively generic with the hope that readers will be able to apply the principles to their unique contexts.

HOMEOSTASIS AND CHANGE (MAINTAINING EQUILIBRIUM AND BALANCE IN THE ENVIRONMENT THROUGH CONSTANT ADAPTATIONS)

It is amazing more things do not go wrong. It is amazing that there are fewer disagreements than might be expected, given the complexity of the communication process. With all the drivers on the road, especially during rush hour in overcrowded cities, it is amazing there are not more accidents. Given humankind's propensity toward self-serving behavior, it is surprising that there are not more crimes or wars. There is a relatively high degree of stability at all levels throughout the universe.

Systems and subsystems emerge over time to establish a semblance of stability and buffering mechanisms to compensate for changes in the environment. Functional and dysfunctional peer groups, families, communities, organizations, local, state, and federal governments, societies, and global partnerships have established stable (and yet temperamental) patterns of social interaction. The metarules and patterns of every system have survived over time, resulting in a state of equilibrium or homeostasis around dominant values unique to the system.

Established systems are relatively resistant. When some changes are thrust upon the system, initially frenetic behavior results, but when the honeymoon period is over, things typically return to the way things were. This is, in part, because the essential characteristics of the system and the infrastructure remain unaltered. Shaking the walls of the chicken coop may initially cause the chickens to run around only eventually to return to their original positions. Many educational initiatives that get implemented do not become institutionalized. Part of the reason is that reform policies that address achievement seldom address the essential features of the system. Students will always be students and teachers will always be teachers. What takes place in the classroom between the students and teachers is relatively impervious to external demands from the different reforms. Teachers and students determine how reform events get implemented.

Paradoxically, homeostasis or stability is achieved through change. The more things change, the more they stay the same. Hence, change at both the macro and micro levels, regardless of the scale of change, is needed and inevitable. Problems that arise can be reframed as symptoms of a system that is out of balance. Problems are interpreted as attempted solutions for the system to maintain some sense of equilibrium.

In the classroom or family living room (or business meeting), a child's (or a business colleague who behaves like a child) acting out is a symptom of something amiss in the larger system: typically that the child's needs and wants are unmet. The child's attempted solution of acting out for attention typically solicits a solution (immediate recognition) and equilibrium is restored. The child's acting out is an indication that his or her agenda is not being met in the system.

As documented in chapter 3, the need for educational reforms surfaces when a particular value is ignored or minimized. Policies are self-corrections to perceived imbalances in the system. At the same time, not all organizational and political problems and agendas are equal. In other words, not all attempted change is good. Some agendas are more self-serving or represent extreme positions that can take the system in a different direction. Various colleagues and constituents clamoring for attention or organizational resources should not necessarily receive equal attention for their respective agendas.

Leaders would do well to anticipate and welcome change as a form of self-correcting behavior within the organization and environment, for, as previously stated, the more things change the more they stay the same. This is not saying all change is good or that leaders need to yield to all changes, lest the system gives way to chaos, but the leader needs to recognize and respond to change in order to keep the organization on course, like any good steersman of a ship. One recent example is the extreme provisions in No Child Left Behind, which was an attempt to correct the erosion of educational standards. No Child Left Behind was in response to the symptom of excellence being minimized at the expense of other priorities. A good steersman would have recognized and anticipated the direction of the wind, so that, if subtle corrections had been made along the way, the extreme measures in NCLB would not have been necessary.

Even with the occasional extreme fluctuations in the organizational and policy patterns, there is an amazing degree of stability over time, relative to the interdependence and interactions among the myriad of variables. Leaders would do well to recognize that the more complex the system, the greater the interdependence the individual parts of the system have in their contribution to the whole and in maintaining equilibrium. This interdependence suggests that there is typically more than one reason for problems and change, and the reasons are typically several layers deep. An example is found when quality control engineers analyze problems or disruptions back to their root cause, typically found around the "fifth why." Appreciating the interdependence of variables, leaders are prudent to ask as many whys as necessary to get to the root cause(s) of a problem.

An example of looking for the root cause in problem solving in organizations is evidenced in the fluctuation of sales experienced by most sales companies. An explosion of sales of a particular product can be easily attributed to an aggressive and capable sales representative. However, sales eventually peak and start to decline. Management easily attributes the change to a decline in the sales representative's performance without additional analysis. But if they ask why sales have dropped, they find customers complained that delivery was slow. When delivery was asked about the slow response pattern, they reported manufacturing was not keeping up with the demand imposed by successful sales. When manufacturing was asked why there is a backup in orders, they could theoretically report from any number of possible scenarios with their own set of whys.

Many educational reforms have been short-sighted because they have not gone back an average of five whys deep in discerning recommendations for the American educational system. When the federal government asks why all students are not achieving the same standards as measured through high stakes testing, analysis stops short with solutions to remedy deficiencies with the states', teachers', parents', and students' standards. Additional analysis might reveal that the question is based upon faulty assumptions.

Why are states and teachers resistant to high stakes testing? Their reply is often that one set of standards is not realistic for all students and high stakes testing leaves little, if any, room in the curriculum for creative reflection and discussion. Why is high stakes testing not realistic for all children? Compulsory education was developed to make schools accessible to all students in the context of industrialization and urbanization, thereby expanding and diversifying the aptitudes, abilities, and motivations represented in each classroom.

Unlike practices in many Asian and European countries, students in America are not presorted according to their aptitudes, abilities, and motivations. One of America's sacred values is individual liberty, which is counter to predetermined sorting for the collective whole. As a result, our system of mass education, as designed, is not suited for universal high stakes testing; it is like forcing a square peg into a round hole (U.S. Department of Education 2003).

Another feature of this stability is that certain factors carry a disproportional amount of influence over the whole system. The ubiquitous 80/20 rule, first credited to the Italian economist Pareto, is evidence of enduring features that give systems relative stability. Pareto surveyed the distribution of wealth and found that 20 percent of the people owned 80 percent of the wealth. Today this rule is seen in corporations in which typically 80 percent of the profit comes from 20 percent of the product (Koch 1999). Churches find that approximately 80 percent of the giving comes from the same 20 percent of the people and approximately 80 percent of the volunteer work is completed by the same 20 percent of the people. In addition, approximately 20 percent of the same people cause about 80 percent of the problems. In schools, 80 percent of student achievement is attributed to student characteristics, while classroom and school characteristics account for 13 percent and 7 percent, respectively (Marzano 2001).

A telling example of the stable qualities established systems possess is found in the common factors research, referenced to as the "Dodo Bird Effect" by Rosenzweig (1936). Rosenzweig recognized that certain common factors at work in various systems are responsible for an inordinate proportion of the outcome. The dodo bird's comment from Lewis Carroll's book *Alice in Wonderland* was, "Everybody has won, and all must have prizes." In psychotherapy, Hubble, Duncan, and Miller (1999) report in their book *The Heart & Soul of Change: What Works in Therapy* that common factors among therapies and therapists are primarily responsible for client improvement. Citing Lambert (1992) as the baseline, the authors provide empirical and qualitative research to support the following common factors at work in any therapeutic relationship.

40 percent: Client and extra therapeutic factors
30 percent: Relationship factors
15 percent: Placebo, hope, and expectancy
15 percent: Model techniques

In essence, 85 percent of the treatment outcomes in therapeutic relationships are associated with factors unrelated to specific treatment techniques. It appears that different therapies appear to be equally effective (every therapy deserves a prize). While differential treatment effects do exist, for the most part, it appears that it is not the particular model of therapy that makes the biggest difference; it is the nature of the client seeking help in the context of a nurturing relationship with the therapist that accounts for the difference (common to all therapeutic modalities). Basically, those who want to get better in life and take steps to get better with life do get better. The therapeutic relationship is the catalyst. It seems someone would get better quicker with a warm and caring, but technically less competent, therapist than with a technically highly competent therapist possessing minimal warmth.

Attending to the critical 20 percent generates disproportional results. A common factor facilitating improvement to the system is introducing some type of change, not the particular method. This point was driven home at a recent international conference on educational leadership. A group of young scholars listening to a panel of experts touting their unique model of school improvement bemoaned that each speaker had his or her own story of success based upon different interventions. What the young scholars (and we suspect the panel of experts) failed to recognize was that it was not the actual method of reform that was making a difference, but rather the fact that people were focusing on making a difference.

The actual commitment and action to improve the system is what leads to improvement, not necessarily a particular intervention. The "silver bullet" of reform is not a universal strategy for all schools and all students, but rather schools implementing an authentic improvement plan.

As already mentioned, the common factor in school achievement is student characteristics (Marzano 2001). Really good (motivated, prepared, and encouraged) students make for really good schools. While really good teachers can facilitate the development of really good students, and for some students, the really good teacher can have an exponential effect (as will be argued later in self-organized criticality, that timing is everything), for the most part, the weight of learning is on the student. As with therapy, a motivated client seeking therapy will probably get better just by seeking out help, regardless of which therapeutic model a counselor uses.

The erroneous conclusion to reach from the dodo bird effect would be to attend to the critical 20 percent and ignore the other 80 percent. To score a 100-yard touchdown, 80 yards will not suffice. Just as there are different portions of the system that have disproportional influence, each part is critical if the system is to work as optimally as possible. At the same time, it is prudent and efficient to attend to the critical 20 percent of the system.

Similar to therapeutic relationships in which approximately 85 percent of the outcome is related to the nature of the relationship, certain types of student-teacher relationships carry a disproportionate weight when it comes to student engagement. How is it that a teacher who relies on lecture can be just as inspiring as those who rely on more engaging learning activities? According to Palmer (1998) and Day (2004), the common factor for excellent teaching is enthusiasm, not correct methods. Teachers who are passionate about the content and their students appear to have a disproportionate effect on student learning than those teachers lacking enthusiasm. Enthusiasm for teaching and learning ushers in a commitment to do what is necessary to get every student to succeed.

Granted, enthusiasm by itself can default into cheerleading, but enthusiasm focused on the mission of student learning compensates for much. It appears that passion covers a multitude of errors in the same tradition that "love covers a multitude of sins" (I Peter 4:8).When people know they are loved, they can tolerate imperfection from their leaders. While the style or methods of parenting, teaching, and leading are important for yielding specific outcomes, supportive relationships contribute disproportionately more to the specific outcomes.

Effective leaders either instinctively or intentionally attend to the vital 20 percent for 80 percent of the desired outcomes. In addition, they normalize that while it may appear 80 percent of the time is spent on problems, at least it only involves 20 percent of the same people or issues. It does not take long to plant and harvest the garden relative to the time it takes to keep the garden weed-free. Leaders need to know their system well enough to know and attend appropriately to the critical 20 percent.

At the same time, leaders need to recognize that if they alter the critical 20 percent in any way, the system can experience a transformational change. The 80/20 rule does not imply a strict 20 percent to 80 percent ratio between the relevant variables but rather reveals a disproportionate impact and outcomes among the various relational variables in the established systems. Some systems are so established that the better rule may be 90/10 (e.g., the federal government supplies approximately 10 percent of the budget for elementary and secondary education, and yet, seems to determine 90 percent of the activity with NCLB's emphasis on high stakes testing).

Leaders need to know their system well so as to identify and activate the appropriate tipping points to effectively achieve desired outcomes. This requires the leader to make appropriate judgment calls and become an expert of the system dynamics in his or her institution and organization. An expert's trained senses notice the subtle nuances and patterns that allow him or her to make more precise assessments and prognostications.

Leadership Principles from Homeostasis and Change

- Anticipate and selectively welcome change.
- Recognize many problems are solutions waiting to happen.
- Evaluate intended and unintended consequences of every potential decision in any given scenario.
- Assess problems for their root cause, typically five whys deep in any given scenario.
- Attend to the 80/20 rule.

STRANGE ATTRACTORS (NONNEGOTIABLES THAT ESTABLISH A RANGE OF ACCEPTABLE LIMITS OF CERTAINTY AND UNCERTAINTY)

The strange attractors give shape and meaning to the system. While welcoming change, leaders must at the same time establish the nonnegotiables for their institution. Not all changes are worthwhile for the system, especially the more heterogeneous the system. Social systems are complex entities and the more participants who connect with the system, the more complex the system becomes. The reason more things go right than wrong is because most members participate according to the strange attractors in the system. Employees do what employers expect, lest they be out of a job. Employers do what employees want, lest they lack employees. Students and teachers make subtle negotiations and compromises in the classroom to reach an appropriate and often unspoken equilibrium. Teachers cannot assign too much homework, lest students resort to mutiny, while students can't refuse to do any homework, lest they fail (Sizer 1984; Powell, Farrar, and Cohen 1985).

Leaders need to recognize that their minimum expectations will typically become the maximum expectations for the group. What leaders attend to and how they attend to it will serve as the strange attractors and define the equilibrium points for the system. Having high expectations and establishing a few nonnegotiables will determine for what the leader and organization are known. In addition, establishing a hierarchy of nonnegotiables (priorities and values) will determine the direction of change. For example, IBM had to change its product from typewriters to personal computers, but retained dedication to quality (nonnegotiable).

Even when the nonnegotiables are established, organizations will have several strange attractors that will compete with each other. Excellence is tempered by efficiency. Justice is tempered by mercy. What is the balance between serving the letter of the law and serving the spirit of the law? The more complex the environment, the more it behooves leaders to establish a range of acceptable behavior to replace rigid ways of doing things.

Giving parameters for latitude allows followers to make judgment calls and respond to the nuances of the immediate context as to which strange attractor is more germane at the moment. Establishing a window of acceptable behavior legitimizes the many competing demands and values in every organization, while at the same time giving priority to certain values over others. The classic example of having a window of tolerance found in education is allowing a range of performance for what is considered passing (grades C or better).

As evident from chapters 2 and 3, America has competing values that mirror themselves in various policies and practices. Excellence, equality, efficiency, and individual freedom are the founding principles (strange attractors) of the United States that are still dominant. Too much of one measure of excellence in education in the form of high stakes testing does a disservice to diversity of learning styles and differential outcomes in an educational system.

Too much emphasis on diversity, though, results in lack of common standards for a nation. Too much emphasis on efficiency can compromise effectiveness and quality. Too much choice in education will potentially create undesirable markets. Public administrators need to maintain a balance between proactive administration, political neutrality, and political responsiveness (Selden, Brewer and Brudney 1999). The more homogeneous the group, the fewer the number of strange attractors at work, making leadership easier in terms of having to make fewer judgment calls. The more heterogeneous the group the more competing values at work, and hence, the more controversial leadership becomes. Finding negotiable values among nonnegotiable values makes leadership complicated.

The presence of competing values in society is evident in that the Supreme Court in the United States has majority and minority opinions over the interpretation of the same laws and facts. Between 1970 and 2004, approximately 39 percent of the decisions garnered unanimous consent of the court while 19 percent of the cases rendered 5–4 split decisions (Epstein et al. 2007). The jurists recognize competing values associated with legal decisions allow for different interpretations and justifications.

Learning from the Supreme Court, leaders would do well to normalize the ambiguity associated with complex decision making by recognizing that the more diverse the issues, the more difficult to reach a unanimous consensus. Leaders need to recognize that in making decisions with equally valid competing values, they have to land somewhere. The classic example in jurisprudence is whether to err on the side of justice or err on the side of mercy. (Two competing values or strange attractors in the justice system are mercy and justice. Justice without mercy is tyranny. Mercy without justice gets perverted to a license to do wrong.)

Administrators also have to discern when to serve the spirit of the law versus the letter of the law. An example of a student being expelled for having a box-cutting tool on campus reveals the downside of a policy for zero tolerance when leaders are neither willing nor courageous to make controversial judgment calls. A high school senior with a 4.0 GPA and from an impoverished background worked at a local grocery store after school stocking shelves. The exemplary student, who did not have one behavioral incident in her file, forgot to remove the box-cutting tool in her pocket from the night before. The principal expelled the student, believing the letter of the law was being served. Fortunately, the school board recognized the spirit of the policy and allowed the student to return to school. Leaders would do well to develop their hierarchy of strange attractors in order to deal with contingencies that will tax their decision making.

In many businesses the dominant strange attractor of maximizing profit competes against some social and ethical responsibilities. One author recalls a business meeting in which the discussion focused on what type of packaging to use for the company's many global products. The decision was eventually made that it was prudent to implement the more costly environmentally friendly packaging in the more environmentally conscious markets and retain the less expensive traditional packaging in specific third world markets. The dominant strange attractor to maximize profit was tempered by what looked good and met consumers' priorities.

In addition to ethics, another suggested nonnegotiable is found in the structure of the Supreme Court. While consensus may not be forthcoming, the process of analyzing a decision with the rigor practiced by the leading jurists provides a sense of justice to each decision. Part of the reason the Supreme Court has credibility is not because of the actual decision made, but because of the due diligence in consulting with each other prior to reaching a majority decision.

This suggests that the integrity of the process of leadership is a powerful strange attractor in maintaining leadership credibility. Most people appear willing to accept decisions they disagree with, if they know there is an ethical why and thorough process behind the decision. In today's society, the capital of trust in the process and leaders is indispensable for group, organizational, and national cohesiveness and consensus. Bosses who behave in a capricious manner may have their decisions implemented, but will lack a loyal following.

Leadership Principles from Strange Attractors

- Determine the nonnegotiables (or strange attractors).
- Develop a hierarchy of nonnegotiables.

- Know when to negotiate nonnegotiables in deference to other nonne-gotiables.
- Tolerate ambiguity, in that many possible right answers may exist in the context of competing values.
- Provide parameters for colleagues to make decisions instead of relying on directives.
- Seek the counsel of others.
- Be ethical. (Integrity, trust, and ethical practices as strange attractors generate disproportionate positive influence on the system.)

FRACTALS (REITERATION OF PATTERNS ACROSS SCALES IN THE ENVIRONMENT)

The various strange attractors are the parameters in which eventual patterns emerge and provide the context for decision making and leadership practices. Fractals, or symmetry across scales, result in the particular values and nonnegotiables to be mirrored throughout the organization and policy environment. As explained in chapters 2 and 3, while each major educational reform has one or two dominant values as the impetus for the particular reform, the remaining values at work in the educational system were also reflected in the individual reforms, just to a lesser degree. NCLB's emphasis on equality and excellence retains features of choice and efficiency in its implementation.

Symmetry across scales teaches that precedents and initial conditions cannot help but reiterate in some type of future manifestation. History cannot help but repeat itself, not because people are bound to forget it, but because future events are reiterations of past events. The same strange attractors that set in motion the values and patterns that established historical events will also usher in future events. Hopefully, though, extreme reiterations of some of history's worst atrocities can be tempered, but unfortunately not eliminated. The leader is now able to anticipate the future as some variation of the past, consistent with the dominant strange attractors. The scale will vary, not necessarily the themes. Organizational and political leaders are also equipped to better calculate the timing and justification for specific policies and changes.

An application of the mirroring effect is for leaders to recognize that their strengths, expectations, and idiosyncrasies will be reiterated throughout the organization. Reiterations of the strange attractors will be manifest at every level of the organization. A leader who requires excellence will eventually see excellence trickle down and flow up. A leader who continually begins meetings late should not be surprised to witness punctuality diminish across all levels of the organization. A leader who collaborates (versus autocratic decision making) will eventually create a collaborative work.

Institutional culture can be transformed in a few years by changing what is attended to, and not attended to, and how things are attended to. The principle of fractals also underscores the importance of ethical leadership, again, because leadership examples and practices eventually mirror themselves throughout the organization. Leaders need to take seriously the moral potency of the commonplace (a nonnegotiable), such that, whatever they attend to and how it is addressed will be reiterated throughout the system.

Leadership Principles from Fractals

- Proactively plan for history to repeat itself as history and future are part of a pattern.
- Recognize that what and how a leader attends to will be mirrored throughout the organization.
- Make a conscious effort to mirror what matters.

CYBERNETICS (CORRECTIVE FEEDBACK TO AND FROM THE ENVIRONMENT)

Feedback is essential and without it systems deteriorate and eventually die. Too much feedback and the system gets overwhelmed and gives way to chaos and eventual collapse; too little feedback will cause the system to starve. In addition, not all feedback is of equal value. Feedback from a chronic complainer or squeaky wheel may contain elements of truth, or feedback from a sycophant may tickle the ears, but, in the end, both only yield limited information. The political arena is especially vulnerable to lopsided feedback. Lobbyists who have means and accessibility disproportionately direct the agendas for policy planning.

A discerning leader is selective as to what feedback he or she solicits and attends to. Strategic feedback provides information on what midcourse corrections need to be implemented consistent with the core values of the nonnegotiables. Feedback from a valued customer is more relevant than feedback from a stranger on the street. Candid feedback from multiple sources is necessary to strategically direct future attention and resources.

Leaders also do well to remember systems emerge and grow in the direction of valued feedback. If leaders continually respond to the squeaky wheel, their organizations will grow or fail in the direction of the noise. If leaders can filter out the appropriate noise and use feedback consistent with their strange attractors, they will grow in the direction consistent with their mission and values. If leaders equally heed every voice clamoring for their attention, their organization will lose its distinctiveness. Leaders who automatically turn the complaint of the day into tomorrow's agenda will be like a rudderless ship. At the same time, if leaders are too selective in what feedback they access, the organization will become unresponsive and rigid, which may lead to its eventual demise.

Instead, leaders need to determine what feedback is critical and then establish the appropriate sensors or mechanisms to hear and interpret the feedback. Leaders would do well to appoint a candid critic who provides alternative explanations to organizational successes and problems. In addition, leaders should implement formal and informal data gathering mechanisms so that data can drive decision making and inform their instincts.

Principals and CEOs benefit from regular debriefing meetings that invite candid and open feedback, in order to be attuned to the fluctuations in the organization and environment so that they can provide necessary midcourse corrections. Systems that run away in the direction of one-sided feedback result in an imbalance, and eventually chaos if a self-correction fails to materialize. It is critical that leaders take on the appropriate steersman role, lest the organization or school or personal politics become tossed back and forth by the wind.

Leaders must not only solicit feedback, but provide relevant feedback along the vertical and horizontal dimensions of their immediate environment. Just as leaders need to make midcourse corrections in their planning, so do people associated with the system. Feedback by definition is reciprocal. Consistent with strange attractors, leaders should solicit and provide feedback regarding mission-critical knowledge. Consistent with fractals, leaders need feedback to flow freely across all levels (or scales), from the micro to the macro level.

The rate and amount of feedback has grown exponentially due to the latest developments in technology. E-mails, the Internet, and cellular technology provide quick feedback from multiple sources that force real-time responses. The policy pendulum will inevitably swing faster now that feedback for self-correction is more accessible and almost instantaneous. The speed and volume of feedback puts new demands and challenges on leaders, such that feedback must be judiciously monitored and evaluated.

Leadership Principles from Cybernetics

- Establish appropriate systems for relevant feedback to flow freely.
- Provide and solicit feedback from a representative sample of colleagues and constituents.
- Vigilantly assess the feedback on the feedback systems.

EMERGENCE (CONTINUAL ADAPTATION TO THE ENVIRONMENT)

While organizational and social systems are relatively stable over time, they are also emerging. Life stories, cities, hurricanes, marriages, mergers, diplomacy, and war are emerging systems that share both similar and unique features with respective counterparts. This uniqueness of each life story, city, marriage, war, and so on is a function of the timing and nature of contemporary events converging with the past to alter the trajectory of future events. Sometimes the contemporary events are out of one's control (like natural disasters) and others are directly in one's control (like whom to marry). A person's first career typically determines where he or she will emerge because different ranges of initial opportunities present themselves accordingly, only to usher in another range of opportunities predicated on what came before. Ethical and unethical decisions are defining moments.

Given the level of complexity and the interdependence of the variables in any one system or subsystem, emergence is a temperamental phenomenon that is ultimately a function of how resilient the system is in relation to the type of change being imposed. This is evident by the fact that companies have different reactions to fluctuations in the stock market and emerge to become what they are the next moment in time, based upon the response patterns and timing.

The federal government emerged from being a nonplayer in education to being a key player in driving educational reform. While the federal government had interest in promoting education since America's founding, prior to 1917 the federal government had a negligible role in education. As the framers of the Constitution took great care in carving out the roles and responsibilities of the federal government, it was no accident that education was noticeably absent from the document. The provision of education was deferred to parents and the states.

It was after the Civil War that a three-person Department of Education was created (1867), which after two years was merged with the Department of the Interior (Cross 2004). In 1917 with the passage of the Smith-Hughes Act, the federal government took an active role in education by providing direct funds to schools for the implementation of vocational arts programs. Once the door was open for federal government to participate in the design of education, subsequent legislation would gradually expand the role of the federal government to the point that the Department of Education gained cabinet-level status in 1979 and now contributes approximately 10 percent of the budget for elementary and secondary education (compared to 0.3 percent of the budget for elementary and secondary education in 1920; Cross 2004). The federal government now yields a disproportionate influence on the system, when considering that its original function was to gather and report statistics for the states.

The implication for leaders in both organizational and political environments is to exercise bold caution in moving forward. Leaders need to give careful attention to intended and unintended consequences of decisions and actions. Each decision will set into motion a chain of events that will directly and indirectly impact future scenarios. A consequence to emergent properties is the slippery slope argument that posits that once a behavior is legitimized it opens the door for more to come.

Leaders need to recognize that precedent setting establishes license and opportunities for new behavioral patterns. Setting the right precedents leads to positive outcomes while setting the wrong precedents can undermine the organization's fidelity to its mission. Each precedent becomes a starting point for future precedents. The slippery slope at work is most evident in the entertainment industry. Promiscuity on television and in the movies has taken on new proportions as the window of what was acceptable and respectable gradually opened over time. What was originally considered socially unacceptable (e.g., bad language or suggestions of nudity and sex) is now permissible and even expected.

At a practical level, the principle of emergence encourages leaders to exercise caution in hiring personnel. People with contrary attitudes and dispositions to the organizational values will either tip the social dynamics or leave because of the mismatch. Either way, valuable resources are used in adjusting to the disruptions associated with employee tension or employee turnover associated with bad hires.

Precedent setting may sound like the slippery slope argument, which is usually summarily dismissed for obfuscating the issues. On the contrary, a holistic picture recognizes that precedent setting determines the new beginning point that becomes a precursor to new patterns. While there is a time for precedent and exceptions, it requires judgment to discern when it is that time. A complexity framework provides the context in which to make an informed judgment call.

Leaders would also do well to rethink traditional long-term strategic planning processes that focus on outcomes and lend themselves to giving a false sense of confidence in the future. Such plans can lead to unresponsiveness to the fluctuations in the environment and missed opportunities. Rather, emergence and complexity science in general suggest leaders develop long-term plans that focus on processes and objectives. Long-term planning requires making judgments about future probabilities while living with a degree of ambiguity because the future is uncertain.

Traditional marketing strategies advocate the development of a five- and ten-year plan based upon projections of the future. Such plans work when the environment and markets cooperate and history and timing are positive. Unfortunately, when such plans are not responsive to the fluctuations in a complex market, they, at times, are positioned to miss opportunities. Organizational leaders and policy planners will do better with an emergent planning model, one that recognizes the dominant values (nonnegotiables) relevant to the system, anticipates probable scenarios accordingly, and appropriately realigns resources on a frequent basis.

Leadership Principles from Emergence

- Boldly and cautiously plan and implement change by evaluating probable intended and unintended consequences.
- Implement emergent planning by conducting long-term planning every year.
- Judiciously choose precedents that serve the dominant values.

SENSITIVE DEPENDENCE ON INITIAL CONDITIONS (BUTTERFLY EFFECT—DISPROPORTIONAL CHANGES IN THE ENVIRONMENT FROM SELECT TRIGGER EVENTS)

The principles of homeostasis reveal that systems are relatively stable. At the same time, some changes have bigger transformational effects than others. Each system has certain tipping points that yield disproportionate influence. Certain small changes can have an inordinate impact on the system. A classic example is the current configuration on computer keyboards. The strategy behind the inefficient placement of letters on the keyboard is the residual of an older technology. The initial typewriters would frequently get stuck as the keys were pressed too fast.

The QWERTY order of keys (top row of letters on the keyboard used by the left hand) was fashioned to force typists to perform at speeds consistent with the technology. The frequently used letters were reassigned to the left hand QWERTY configuration so that typists would be forced to slow down their speed, resulting in less keys being stuck. Now with computers and electronic keyboards, the issue of stuck keys is moot. While new keyboard configurations for the letters have been designed to increase typing speed, such keyboards have not been implemented due to people's resistance to retool and the established networks built around the traditional keyboard configuration.

Some imprints or initial conditions can actually constrain future innovation. The egg-crate infrastructure of schools, with the accompanying bell schedule and Carnegie unit of instruction, limits what and how reforms get implemented in the classroom. Change that does not target some of the assumptions behind the initial conditions will have minimal impact. To take advantage of sensitive dependence on initial conditions, educational reform that centers on getting the right type of teachers in the classroom will have a disproportionate impact on student achievement, more so than other reforms that ignore issues of the existing infrastructure of schools (e.g., substantive increase in teacher salaries).

Legitimizing school vouchers and choice is one example of a radical educational reform that could change the nature of the system and overcome constraints imposed by the existing infrastructure imprinted on the educational system. Driven by market forces (e.g., students, parents, teachers, and community members), schools can be redesigned to fit the needs and desires of the various constituent groups (to be competitive) and the comprehensive needs and values of the societies in which they are members (the schools' niche). The result is the shedding of the constraining vestiges of a system designed for the previous century. Choice-based reforms equally allow individuals to efficiently pursue excellent learning opportunities consistent with his or her abilities and predispositions.

Leaders need to know their system well so as to identify and activate the appropriate tipping points to effectively achieve desired outcomes. This requires the leader to be an expert of the system dynamics in his or her institution and organization. The expert's trained senses to discern the subtle nuances and patterns in the system equip him or her to make wise decisions.

It is important to note that not all initial conditions are equal. Some initial conditions are more consequential, a function of the organizing conditions of the system and how temperamental the system is. How is it that a smile, a kind word, or a simple courtesy can change the outcome of someone's day? How is it that a lady by the name of Rosa Parks, by refusing to give up her seat on a bus, becomes a catalyst for a large-scale social movement? How is it that one enthusiastic and encouraging teacher can transform a lethargic student into a motivated student? Gladwell (2002), in his book *The Tipping Point*, recounts various social situations in which a strategically small change brings about a disproportionate range of consequences, such as fixing broken windows being attributed to a decline in crime. The leader needs to know the system well enough in order to discern what those significant changes could be.

Leadership Principles from Sensitive Dependence

• Recognize that certain small changes can have a big effect.
• Recognize that certain big changes can have a small effect.

SELF-ORGANIZED CRITICALITY (TEMPERAMENTAL INTERDEPENDENCE WITH THE ENVIRONMENT)

Ideal performance looks good on paper and in theory, but leadership is messy and the most that leaders can hope for is the "best possible state [not the ideal state] that is dynamically achievable" (Bak 1996, 198). Leaders need to again make sure they are vigilant in nurturing and attending to the critical elements of the system. At the same time, it behooves leaders to have contingency plans while recognizing that even the best prevention and proactive planning cannot always prevent a minor situation from cascading into a larger situation.

Variables can converge in such a way that an isolated event triggers a cascade of expected and unexpected events, that the combination of such events becomes more consequential than if the events happened in isolation (i.e., the cascading sand pile referenced in chapter 1). While perfect storms are relatively rare, they happen, and, to some degree, are out of a leader's control. Unfortunately, there are perfect storms in which variables converge such that under other circumstances, the impact would not have been as great. Stanislow (2005) captures the similar wisdom that timing is almost everything when he observes that "No snowflake in an avalanche ever feels responsible" (cited in Geary 2005, 190).

The timing of events in relational environments makes for temperamental situations. The educational system is at risk of being overwhelmed at any point in time given the amount and rate of feedback and the plethora of expectations on education. Given the current state of complexity, it is amazing that the educational system has not yet imploded or bifurcated.

As evident from chapters 2 and 3, no single reform has yet to attend equally to the issues of excellence, choice, equality, and efficiency. As a result, the system is in jeopardy of becoming something radically different. Advances in online learning may well minimize the number of actual schools or universities currently in the system, if not make the bricks and mortars completely obsolete. The growth of choice programs is evidence that the system may be approaching a point of self-organized criticality to become a system consisting of multiple systems.

Self-organized criticality teaches that control is elusive and that leaders would do well to plan for the best (rules of homeostatic and emerging systems), but prepare for the worst (self-organized criticality). In addition, when it comes to leadership planning, self-organized criticality also teaches that there is no guarantee that a leader's previous success will transfer to the next activity or placement. Successful performance is always, in part, contingent upon the combination of the leader's activity and the variables in the immediate context. The requisite humility required of effective leaders is easily maintained when leaders recognize that timing and history matter, and that success is, in part, attributed to being at the right place at the right time. Chance seems to favor a prepared person. Often leaders recognize that fate played a partial role in their rise to the top (Shoup 2005).

Leadership Principles from Self-Organized Criticality

- Plan for the best and prepare for the worst.
- Remember that timing is critical.

REFRAMING

At this point an eighth principle that logically follows from a systemic orientation is offered. Prior to the advent of systems and complexity theory, leaders would typically assess scenarios as if their observations and explanatory schema were objective and independent from the situation. The reality of nonlinear systems requires people to recognize that they are part of the system; hence, their assessments are not automatically objective and do influence how the system behaves in turn. Leaders inadvertently create and perpetuate problems they attempt to solve for lack of recognition that their framing of the problems and solutions becomes embedded in the system.

For example, if a leader labels an overly zealous colleague as adversarial, versus passionate, he or she risks creating an adversarial relationship. Future interactions are tainted as the defensive behavior of the leader solicits defensive behavior from the colleague that leads to an adversarial dynamic, without the leader realizing that he or she has created a self-fulfilling prophecy. Politicians who label opponents as "foe" versus "colleague" solicit different response patterns. Leaders need to recognize they are part of the system and create specific social realities by their respective response patterns.

Systemic thinking provides alternative interpretations to problems and opportunities. A systemic perspective also enables leaders to strategically reframe issues to leverage relevant characteristics for desired outcomes. Systemic thinkers recognize the multiple patterns and themes at work in any given situation and, therefore, are better equipped to appeal to the more germane pattern, sometimes the transcendent pattern, for optimal solutions.

Watzlawick, Weakland, and Fisch (1974) illustrate the power of reframing made possible by systemic thinking with the following story.

> During one of the many nineteenth-century riots in Paris the commander of an army detachment received orders to clear a city square by firing at the *canaille* (rabble). He commanded his soldiers to take up firing positions, their rifles leveled at the crowd; as a ghastly silence descended he drew his sword and shouted at the top of his lungs: "Mesdames, m'sieurs, I have orders to fire at the *canaille*. But as I see a great number of honest, respectable citizens before me, I request that they leave so that I can safely shoot the *canaille*." The square was empty in a few minutes. . . . The officer is faced with a threatening crowd. In a typical first-order change fashion he has instructions to oppose hostility with counter-hostility, with more of the same. Since his men are armed and the crowd is not, there is little doubt that "more of the same" will succeed. But in the wider context this change would not only be no change, it would further inflame the existing turmoil. Through his intervention the officer effects a second-order change—he takes the situation outside the frame that up to that moment contained both him and the crowd; he reframes it in a way acceptable to everyone involved,

and with this reframing both the original threat and its threatened "solution" can safely be abandoned. (81–82)

Reframing has the possibility of de-escalating many conflicts and creating possibilities. A classic example of reframing is used to help some disillusioned marriage partners notice patterns they are missing. Each partner is told to do five secret things for his or her spouse and return the next week to report if they can recognize the five things. The couple returns with the presenting symptom reduced. When asked to guess the mysterious five nice things that his or her spouse did for them, the partner often recalls ten additional items the spouse had always done but went unnoticed because of the preexisting mind-set. Secretly reframing what to look for typically leads couples to recognize what was always there by changing the focus to other patterns in the system.

Parents who reframe a student's complaint that twenty minutes of homework is too much to "you only have twenty minutes of homework, I better talk to your teacher" automatically curb the sense of injustice and make additional conversations moot. Reframing educational reform from a particular fad to some type of self-correction in the larger contest of values helps to legitimize the swinging pendulum of reform.

Another poignant example on the power of thinking outside the box by using a paradoxical reframe is found in an interesting interaction that involved Khrushchev and the defection of Stalin's daughter Svetlanka as recorded by Khrushchev (Khrushchev 1970). After complaining how wrong it had been for her to defect, Khrushchev suggests how the defection could have been possibly avoided with a different form of rhetoric.

She did something stupid, but Svetlanka was dealt with stupidly, too—stupidly and rudely. Apparently, after her husband's funeral she went to our embassy in New Delhi. Benediktov was our ambassador there. I knew him. He's a very straight-laced person. Svetlanka said she wanted to stay in India for a few months, but Benediktov advised her to return immediately to the Soviet Union. This was stupid on his part. When a Soviet ambassador recommends that a citizen of the Soviet Union return home immediately, it makes the person suspicious. Svetlanka was particularly familiar with our habits in this regard. She knew it meant she wasn't trusted.

What do I think should have been done? I'm convinced that if she had been treated differently, the regrettable episode would never have happened: When Svetlanka came to the embassy and said that she had to stay in India for two or three months, they should have told her, "Svetlanka Iosifovna, why only three months? Get a visa for a year or two or even three years. You can get a visa and live here. Then, whenever you are ready, you can go back to the Soviet Union." If she had been given freedom of choice, her morale would have been boosted. They should have shown her that she was trusted. . . . And what if we had acted the way I think we should have and Svetlanka still hadn't returned home from India? Well, that would have been too bad but no worse than what happened. (294–95)

Not only does reframing alter social realities, how people respond can have a tremendous impact on a situation. The classic example of a leader's response altering outcomes is found in Proverbs 15:1, "A gentle word turns away wrath but a harsh word stirs up anger." The de-escalation or escalation of conflict is in part predicated on the trust and tone leaders develop and utilize.

Leadership Principles from Reframing

- Recognize respective roles in the system in creating the social realities that emerge.
- Reframe problems and solutions to leverage the most appropriate and relevant theme(s) and patterns at work in the system.

SUMMARY AND CONCLUSION

Two premises of this book are that leadership matters and it matters to an *nth* degree more in an already complex world. The accelerating rate of change and the speed of communication in an ever-expanding ethnically, culturally, and religiously diverse society suggests complexity will only increase. Complex systems consist of a myriad of interactions with a myriad of variables. Anomalies to the norm "randomly" appear (a fatal accident, a birth defect, a plane crash, epidemics, stock market crashes, bankruptcies, hurricanes, etc.), suggesting that there is amazing order in the universe at both the macro and micro levels.

Given the level of complexity confronting society, it is amazing how many things go right given all that could go wrong. The simple rules outlined throughout this book, when kept in balance, allow complexity to work without giving way to chaos. At one level, while it appears people are managing chaos, it is recognized that, at any one point, the system could collapse into chaos. Complexity science has captured the intricacies of nature, providing an avenue for understanding the complexities of nature and institutional life.

The suggestions for leadership practices sound contradictory—establish and negotiate your nonnegotiables; maintain stability, but embrace change; plan for the best, but prepare for the worst; attend to the small things for biggest effect; be cautiously bold when implementing change; judiciously welcome feedback, but not too much nor too little; and treat problems as solutions waiting to happen. This is the fate of leadership in complex environments and why much of leadership is about making judgment calls in the context of ambiguity.

Those attuned to the intricacies of specific institutional systems and the general principles of complexity science are the ones equipped to successfully navigate the emerging and dynamic future. Being prepared and understanding the nature of the system gives today's leaders the advantage necessary to lead in today's complicated world. Using the guidelines presented in this book disentangles some of the mystery of being a leader in the twenty-first century.

References

Adamic, L. A. 2000. *Power-laws and Pareto: A ranking tutorial.* Palo Alto, CA. Xerox Palo Alto Research Center.

Aikin, W. 1942. *The story of the Eight-Year Study.* New York: Harper & Row.

American Educational Research Association. 2010. *Chaos and complexity theories (SIG #17).* Retrieved February 1, 2010, from www.aera.net/SIGs/Sig Directory.aspx?menu_id=26&id=4714.

Ampere, A. M. 1834. *Essai sur la philosophie des science* (Essay on the philosophy of science). Paris: Chez Bachelier.

Ashby, W. R. 1956. *An introduction to cybernetics.* London: Chapman & Hall.

Bak, P. 1996. *How nature works: The science of self-organized criticality.* New York: Copernicus.

Barabasi, A. L., and E. Bonabeau. 2003. Scale-free networks. *Scientific American* 288, no. 5: 60–70.

Beale, D. 1998. The rise and fall of Harvard (1636–1805). *DBSJ* 3, no. 1: 89–101.

Berman, D. M. 1966. *It is so ordered: The Supreme Court rules on school segregation.* New York: W.W. Norton & Company.

Bestor, A. 1953/1985. *Educational wastelands: The retreat from learning in our public schools,* 2nd ed. Chicago: University of Illinois Press.

Betts, J. R., and T. Loveless. 2005. *Getting choice right.* Washington, DC: The Brookings Institution.

Biennial Survey of Education in the United States. 1921. Washington, DC: Government Printing Office.

Bilingual Education Act. 1968. 20 U.S.C. 3283(a)(1).

Birnbaum, R. 1988. *How colleges work: The cybernetics of academic organization and leadership.* San Francisco: Jossey-Bass.

Boleman, L., and T. Deal. 2003. *Reframing organizations: Artistry, choice, and leadership*, 3rd ed. San Francisco: Jossey-Bass.

Brimley, V., and R. R. Garfield. 2005. *Financing education in a climate of change*, 9th ed. Boston: Allyn & Bacon.

Brint, S. 2006. *Schools and societies*, 2nd ed. Stanford, CA: Stanford University Press.

Brown v. Board of Education. 1954. 347 U.S. 483.

——. 1955. 349 U.S. 294.

Buchanan, M. 2000. *Ubiquity: Why catastrophes happen*. New York: Three Rivers Press.

——. 2001. *Ubiquity: The science of history or why the world is simpler than we think*. London: Weidenfeld & Nicolson.

Cawelti, G. 2006 (November). The side effects of NCLB. *Educational Leadership* 64, no. 3: 64–68.

Center for Education Reform. 2009. *National charter school & enrollment statistics 2009*. Retrieved February 1, 2010, from www.edreform.com/_upload/CER_charter_numbers.pdf.

Chronicle of Higher Education. 2009. Almanac Issue 2009–10, LVI: 1.

Cohen, A. M., and F. B. Brawer. 1989. *The American community college*. San Francisco: Jossey-Bass.

Committee of the Corporation and the Academical Faculty. 1828. *Reports on the course of instruction in Yale College*. New Haven, CT: Hezekiah Howe.

Coolidge, C. 1925 (January). *The press under a free government*. Speech presented at American Society of Newspaper Editors, Washington, DC.

Cousin, M. V. 1835. *Report on the state of education in Prussia; Addressed to the Count De MontAlivet, Peer of France, Minister of Public Instruction and Ecclesiastical Affairs*. Trans. S. Austin. New York: Wiley & Long.

Crawford, J. 1991. *Bilingual education: History and politics theory and practice*. Los Angeles: Bilingual Education Services.

Cremin, L. 1957. *The republic and the school: Horace Mann on the education of free men*. New York: Teachers College.

Cross, C. 2004. The U.S. Department of Education at 25: A history remembered. *Education Week* 24, no. 8: 40–42.

Cuban, L. 2003. *Oversold and underused: Computers in the classroom*. Cambridge, MA: Harvard University Press.

Cubberley, E. P. 1920/1922. *The history of education*. Cambridge, MA: The Riverside Press.

Cusick, P. A. 1992. *The educational system: Its nature and logic*. New York: McGraw-Hill.

Day, C. 2004. *A passion for teaching*. London: Routledge Falmer.

de Tocqueville, A. 1835/1984. *Democracy in America.* New York: Mentor.

Dewey, J. 1900/1902. *The school and society/The child and the curriculum.* Chicago: The University of Chicago Press.

———. 1935/1938. *Experience & education.* New York: Touchstone.

Diener, T. 1986. *Growth of an American invention: A documentary history of the junior and community college movement* (Contributions to the Study of Education, No. 16). Westport, CT: Greenwood.

Eidenberg, E., and R. D. Morey. 1969. *An act of Congress: The legislative process and the making of education policy.* New York: W.W. Norton & Company.

Eleanor Roosevelt Papers Project. 2003. *The progressive era.* Retrieved July 30, 2009, from www.gwu.edu/~erpapers.

Elementary and Secondary Education Act. 1965. Public Law 89-1.

Epstein, L., J. A. Segal, H. J. Spaeth, and T. G. Walker. 2007. *The Supreme Court compendium: Data, decisions & developments.* Washington DC: CQ Press.

Fields, R. 1962. *The community college movement.* New York: McGraw-Hill.

Friedman, T. L. 2005. *The World is flat: A brief history of the twenty-first century.* New York: Farrar, Straus, Giroux.

Fuhrman, S., and M. Lazerson. 2005. *American institutions of democracy: The public schools* (Institutions of American Democracy Series). New York: Oxford University Press.

Fullan, M. 2001. *Leading in a culture of change.* San Francisco: Jossey-Bass.

Gaither, M. 2008. *Homeschool: An American history.* New York: Palgrave Macmillan.

Gardner, J. W. 1990. *On leadership.* New York: The Free Press.

Geary, J. 2005. *The word in a phrase: A brief history of the aphorism.* New York: Bloomsbury Publishing.

Gibbs, N. 2005. Parents behaving badly: Inside the new classroom power struggle: What teachers say about pushy moms and dads who drive them crazy. *Time* (February 21): 40–49.

Gladwell, M. 2002. *The tipping point: How little things can make a big difference.* New York: Little, Brown and Company.

Gleick, J. 1987. *Chaos: Making a new science.* New York: Penguin Books.

Goldin, C., and L. F. Katz. 2008 (December). *Why the United States led in education: Lessons from secondary school expansion, 1910 to 1940.* Paper presented at a Rochester Conference in honor of Stanley Engerman.

Goldstein, J. 2008. Conceptual foundations of complexity science. In *Complexity leadership part I: Conceptual foundations,* ed. M. Uhl-Bien and R. Marion, 17–48. Charlotte, NC: Information Age Publishing.

Government Spending in the United States of America. 2010. *United States federal, state and local government spending.* Retrieved February 11, 2010, from www.usgovernmentspending.com/year2006_0.html#usgs302.

Guthrie, J., and M. Springer. 2004. Returning to square one: From Plessy to Brown and back to Plessy. *Peabody Journal of Education* 79, no. 2: 5–32.

Haas, E., G. Wilson, C. Cobb, and S. Rallis. 2005. One hundred percent proficiency: A mission impossible. *Equity & Excellence in Education* 38: 180–189.

Halperin, S. 1975. ESEA ten years later. *Educational Researcher* 4, no. 8: 5–9.

Hansen, D. 1993. From role to person: The moral layeredness of classroom teaching. *American Educational Research Journal* 30, no. 4: 651–74.

Harper, W. R. 1901/1986. University Record, V (April 6, 1900–March 29, 1901), Chicago: University of Chicago. In *Growth of an American invention: A documentary history of the junior and community college movement* (Contributions to the Study of Education, No. 16), ed. T. Diener, 12–13. Westport, CT: Greenwood.

Harvard Law Review Association. 2009. Church, choice, and charters: A new wrinkle for public education? *Harvard Law Review* 122: 1750–71.

Heylighen, F., and C. Joslyn. 1992. What is systems theory? In *Principia Cybernetica Web*, ed. F. Heylighen, C. Joslyn, and V. Turchin. Brussels: Principia Cybernetica. Retrieved January 26, 2010, from pespmc1.vub.ac.be/SYSTHEOR.html.

Higher Education Act of 1965. 1965. Public Law No. 89-329.

Hilborn, R. C. 1994. *Chaos and nonlinear dynamics: An introduction for scientist and engineers.* New York: The Guilford Press.

Hill, D. M., and M. Barth. 2004. NCLB and teacher retention: Who will turn out the lights? *Education and the Law* 16: 173–81.

Hubble, M. A., B. L. Duncan, and S. D. Miller. 1999. *The heart and soul of change.* Washington, DC: American Psychological Association.

Hutcheson, P. 2007. The Truman Commission's vision of the future. *Thought & Action* 23: 107–15.

Institute for the Study of Coherence and Emergence. 2010. Why E:CO? Retrieved February 1, 2010, from iscepublishing.com/ECO/why_eco.aspx.

Jackson, M. 2000. *Systems approaches to management.* New York: Kluwer Academic.

Jernegan, M. 1918. Compulsory education in the American colonies: I. New England. *The School Review* 26, no. 10: 731–49.

Jischke, M. 2004 (November 16). *Adapting Justin Morrill's vision to a new century: The imperative of change for land-grant universities.* Lecture delivered at the 117th annual meeting of the National Association of State Universities and Land Grant Colleges, San Diego, CA.

Johnson, L. B. 1964a. *Annual message to the Congress on the state of the union.* Retrieved November 26, 2008, from www.lbjlib.utexas.edu/johnson/archives .hom/speeches.hom/640108.asp.

————. 1964b. *Remarks in Providence at the 200th Anniversary Convocation of Brown University.* Retrieved November 26, 2008, from www.presidency.ucsb .edu/ws/index.php?pid=26534.

Jones, A. 1918. Are our schools Prussian in origin? *Education Review* 41: 271–94.

Kafer, K. 2009. *A chronology of school choice in the U.S.* Golden, CO: Independence Institute.

Keeney, B. P. 1983. *Aesthetics of change.* New York: The Guilford Press.

Kiel, D. L., and E. Elliott, eds. 1997. *Chaos theory in the social sciences: Foundations and applications.* Ann Arbor: University of Michigan Press.

Khrushchev, N. 1970. *Khrushchev remembers,* trans. T. Strobe. Boston: Little Brown and Company.

Kliebard, H. M. 1995. *The struggle for the American curriculum: 1893–1958.* New York: Routledge.

————. 1999. *Schooled to work: Vocationalism and the American curriculum: 1876–1946.* New York: Teachers College Press.

————. 2002. *Changing course: American curriculum reform in the 20th century.* New York: Teachers College Press.

Koch, R. 1999. *The 80/20 principle: The secret to success by achieving more with less.* New York: Doubleday.

Koos, L. 1925. *The junior college movement.* Boston: Ginn and Company.

Kridel, C., and R. Bullough. 2007. *Stories of the Eight-Year Study: Reexamining secondary education in America.* Albany: State University of New York Press.

Kuhn, T. 1970. *The structure of scientific revolutions,* 2nd ed. Chicago: The University of Chicago Press.

Lambert, M. 1992. Implications for outcome research for psychotherapy integration. In *Handbook of psychotherapy integration,* ed. J. C. Norcross and M. R. Goldstein, 94–129. New York: Basic Books.

Lancaster, J. 1805. *Improvements in education as it respects the industrious classes of the community,* 3rd ed. London: Kessinger Publishing.

Lannie, V. P., and B. C. Diethorn. 1968. For the honor and glory of God: The Philadelphia Bible riots of 1840. *History of Education Quarterly* 8, no. 1: 44–106.

Lazonick, W. 2005. *American corporate economy: Critical perspectives on business and management.* Oxford, UK: Taylor & Francis.

Lemann, N. 2000. *The big test: The secret history of the American meritocracy.* New York: Farrar, Straus, Giroux.

Leslie, J. B., and E. V. Velsor. 1996. *A look at derailment today: North America and Europe.* Greensboro, NC: Center for Creative Leadership.

Lips, D. 2008. School choice: Policy developments and national participation estimates in 2007–2008. *Backgrounder* 2102 (January 31), 1–12.

Lorenz, E. D. 1993. *The essence of chaos.* Seattle: University of Washington Press.

Lucas, C. J. 1994. *American higher education: A history.* New York: St. Martin's Griffen.

Malone, D. M. 2002. *A brief history of the United States Department of Education 1979–2002.* Durham, NC: Center for Child & Family Policy, Duke University.

Mann, H. 1848/1957. *The republic and the school.* New York: Teachers College Press.

Marion, R. 1999. *The edge of organization: Chaos and complexity theories of formal social systems.* Thousand Oaks, CA: SAGE Publications.

———. 2008. Complexity theory for organizations and organizational leadership. In *Complexity leadership part I: Conceptual foundations*, ed. M. Uhl-Bien and R. Marion, 1–15. Charlotte, NC: Information Age Publishing.

Marshall, C., D. Mitchell, and F. Wirt. 1989. *Culture and education policy in the American states.* New York: The Falmer Press.

Martin, R. 2007. How successful leaders think. *Harvard Business Review* 85 (June): 60–67.

Marzano, R. J. 2001. *A new era of school reform: Going where the research takes us.* Aurora, CO: Mid-continent Research for Education and Learning.

McGuinn, P. J. 2006. *No Child Left Behind and the transformation of federal education policy, 1965–2005.* Lawrence: University Press of Kansas.

McKim, D. 2007. Point of view: The road less traveled. *Phi Delta Kappan* (December): 298–99.

Mettler, S. 2005. The creation of the G.I. Bill of Rights of 1944: Melding social and participatory citizenship ideals. *The Journal of Policy History* 17: 345–74.

Meyer, J., D. Tyack, J. Nagel, and A. Gordon. 1979. Public education as nation-building in America: Enrollments and bureaucratization in the American states, 1870–1930. *The American Journal of Sociology* 85, no. 3: 591–613.

Morrill Act. 1862. ch. 130, 12 Stat. 503, 7 U.S.C. 301 et seq.

Morrison, K. 2002. *School leadership and complexity theory.* New York: Routledge Falmer.

National Association of State Universities and Land Grant Colleges. 1995. *The
Land-Grant tradition.* Washington, DC: Author.

National Center for Education Statistics. 1993. *120 years of American education:
A statistical portrait.* Washington, DC: U.S. Department of Education.

———. 2008a. *1.5 million homeschooled students in the United States in 2007.*
Washington, DC: U.S. Department of Education.

———. 2008b. *Percentage of persons age 25 and over and 25 to 29, by race/
ethnicity, years of school completed, and sex: Selected years, 1910 through
2007.* Retrieved September 18, 2008, from nces.ed.gov/programs/digest/d07/
tables/dt07_008.asp.

———. 2009. *Characteristics of private schools in the United States: Results from
the 2007–08 private school universe survey.* Washington, DC: U.S. Department of Education.

National Commission on Excellence in Education. 1984. *A nation at risk: The full
account.* Portland, OR: USA Research.

National Defense Education Act. 1958. Public Law 85-864, pp. 1580–1605.

National Education Association. 1894. *Report of the Committee of the Ten on
secondary school studies, with the reports of the conferences arranged by the
committee.* New York: American Book Company.

———. 1918. *Cardinal principles of secondary education.* Washington, DC:
Government Printing Office.

National Vocational Education (Smith-Hughes) Act. 1917. Public Law No. 347,
S. 703 Sec 1.

Nichols, S. L., and D. C. Berliner. 2008a. Why has high-stakes testing so easily
slipped into contemporary American life? *The Education Digest* (December):
41–47.

———. 2008b. Testing the joy out of learning. *Educational Leadership* 65, no.
6, 14–18.

No Child Left Behind Act. 2001/2002. Public Law 107-110.

Nutt, P. C. 2002. *Why decisions fail: Avoiding the blunder and traps that lead to
debacles.* San Francisco: Berrett-Koehler Publishers.

Office of Education. 1938. *Bulletin 1938, No. 6, Offerings and registrations in
high school subjects, 1933–34.* Washington, DC: United States Government
Printing Office.

———. 1948. *Life adjustment education for every youth.* Washington, DC: United
States Government Printing Office.

O'Scannlain, D. 2007. The curious case of free exercise. *First Things First: A
Monthly Journal of Religion & Public Life* 178: 35–40.

Osgood, R. L. 2005. *The history of inclusion in the United States.* Washington, DC: Gallaudet University Press.

Pak, M. 2008. Yale report of 1828: A new reading and new implications. *History of Education Quarterly* 48: 30–57.

Palmer, P. 1998. *The courage to teach: Exploring the inner landscape of a teacher's life.* San Francisco: Jossey-Bass.

Parsons, S., and A. Harrington. 2009. Following the script. *Phi Delta Kappan* 90: 748–50.

Peck, S. 1978. *The road less traveled: A new psychology of love, traditional values and spiritual growth.* New York: A Touch Stone Book.

Pierce v. Society of Sisters. 1925. 268 U.S. 510.

Planty, M., W. Hussar, T. Snyder, S. Provasnik, G. Kena, R. Dinkes, A. Kewal-Ramani, and J. Kemp. 2008. *The condition of education 2008* (NCES 2008-031). Washington, DC: National Center for Education Statistics, Institute of Education Sciences, U.S. Department of Education.

Plessy v. Ferguson. 1896. 163 U.S. 53.

Powell, A. G., E. Farrar, and D. K. Cohen. 1985. *The shopping mall high school: Winners and losers in the educational marketplace.* Boston: Houghton Mifflin Company.

President's Commission on Higher Education. 1947. Organizing higher education. In *Growth of an American invention: Documentary history of the junior and community college movement* (Contributions to the Study of Education, No. 16), ed. T. Diener, 5–15. Westport, CT: Greenwood.

Ravitch, D. 2000. *The great school wars: A history of the New York City public schools.* Baltimore: John Hopkins University Press.

———. 2001. *Left back: A century of battles over school reform.* New York: Touchstone Books.

Reich, R. 2009. Government in your business. *Harvard Business Review* (July–August): 94–99.

Representative Rhode (AZ). 1965. "Elementary and Secondary Education Act of 1965." *Congressional Record* 3, no. 5 (March 24): H5766.

Representative Smith (VA). 1965. "Elementary and Secondary Education Act of 1965." *Congressional Record* 3, no. 5 (March 24): H5729.

Rickover, H. G. 1959. *Education and freedom.* New York: E. P. Dutton & Co.

Roosevelt, T. R. 1903 (September 7). *The square deal.* Retrieved from www.theodore-roosevelt.com/trsquaredealspeech.html.

Rosenzweig, S. 1936. Some implicit common factors in diverse methods of psychotherapy. *American Journal of Orthopsychiatry* 6: 412–15.

Ruderman, M., and P. Ohlott. 1994. *The realities of management promotion: An investigation of factors influencing the promotion of managers in three major companies.* Greensboro, NC: Center for Creative Leadership.

Sacks, P. 1999. *Standardized minds: The high price of America's testing culture and what we can do to change it.* Cambridge, MA: Perseus.

Sanders, T. I., and J. A. McCabe. 2003. *The uses of complexity science: A survey of federal department and agencies, private foundations, universities, and independent education and research centers.* Washington, DC: Washington Center for Complexity & Public Policy.

Schneider, M., P. Teske, and M. Marschall. 2000. *Choosing schools: Consumer choice and the quality of American schools.* Princeton, NJ: Princeton University Press.

Selden, S. C., G. A. Brewer, and J. L. Brudney. 1999. Reconciling competing values in public administration. *Administration & Society* 31, no. 2: 171–204.

Senator Morse (OR). 1965. "Elementary Secondary Education Act of 1965." *Congressional Record* 3, no. 6 (April 7): S7317.

Senator Williams (DE). 1965. "Elementary Secondary Education Act of 1965." *Congressional Record* 3, no. 6 (April 9): S7710.

Shedd, J. 2003. The history of the student credit hour. *New Directions for Higher Education* 122: 5–12.

Shoup, J. 2005. *A collective biography on twelve world-class leaders: A study on developing exemplary leaders.* Lanham, MD: University of America Press.

Sizer, T. 1984. *Horace's compromise: The dilemma of American high schools.* New York: Houghton Mifflin Company.

Slawson, D. 2005. *The Department of Education battle, 1918–1932: Public schools, Catholic schools, and the social order.* Notre Dame, IN: University of Notre Dame.

Smith, A. 1776. *An inquiry into the nature and causes of the wealth of nations.* London: Random House.

Sniegoski, S. J. 1988. *A bibliography of the literature on the history of the U.S. Department of Education and its forerunners.* Washington, DC: Department of Education (ERIC Document Reproduction Service No. ED304394).

Spradlin, T. E., and K. A. Prendergast. 2006. *Emerging trends in teacher recruitment and retention in the No Child Left Behind era.* Bloomington, IN: Center for Evaluation & Educational Policy, Indiana University.

Stout, R. T., M. Tallerico, and K. P. Scribner. 1994. Values: The "what?" of the politics of education. In *The Study of Educational Politics*, ed. J. D. Scribner and D. Layton, 1–17. Washington DC: Falmer Press.

Swinton, L. 2009. *Process improvement made easy: Root cause analysis in action.* Retrieved August 9, 2009, from www.mftrou.com/support-files/root-cause-analysis-example.pdf.

Taylor, F. W. 1911. *The principles of scientific management.* New York: Harper & Brothers Publishers.

Thelin, J. R. 2004. *A history of American higher education*. Baltimore: The Johns Hopkins University Press.

Title IX. 1972. Education Amendments of 1972, 20 USC § 1681.

Tyack, D. B. 1974. *The one best system: A history of American urban education.* Cambridge, MA: Harvard University Press.

Tyack, D., and W. Tobin. 1994. The "grammar" of schooling: Why has it been so hard to change? *American Educational Research Journal* 31, no. 3: 453–79.

Uhl-Bien, M., and R. Marion, eds. 2008. *Complexity leadership, part I: Conceptual foundations*. Charlotte, NC: Information Age Publishing.

Urban, W. J., and J. L. Wagoner Jr. 2004. *American education: A history*. New York: McGraw-Hill.

U.S. Department of Education. 2003. USA Research, Inc. 1984. *A nation at risk: The full account*. Portland, OR: Author.

———. 2008. *Nonpublic education: A vital part of U.S. K–12 education*. Washington, DC: Author.

Viteritti, J. 2001. *Choosing equality: School choice, the constitution, and civil society*. Washington, DC: The Brookings Institution.

von Bertalanffy, L. 1968. *General systems theory*. Retrieved January 26, 2010, from www.panarchy.org/vonbertalanffy/systems.1968.html.

Wakefield, D. 2007. NCLB keeps some great teaching candidates out forever. *The Education Digest* (January): 51–57.

Watzlawick, P. D., J. Weakland, and R. Fisch. 1974. *Change: Principles of problem formations and problem resolution*. New York: W.W. Norton & Company.

Weaver, W. 1948. Science and complexity. *American Scientist* 36: 536.

Wheatley, M. 1997. *Leadership and the new science: Discovering order in a chaotic world*. San Francisco: Berrett-Koehler.

Wiener, N. 1948/1961. *Cybernetics: Or control and communication in the animal and the machine*. Cambridge, MA: The MIT Press.

Williams, J. 2004. The ruling that changed. *American School Board Journal* 191: 18–21.

Zook, G. F. 1948. *Higher education for American democracy: A report of the President's Commission on Higher Education*. New York: Harper & Brothers.

Index

Note: Figures and tables are indicated by "f" or "t" following the page number.

Addams, Jane, 43
adequate yearly progress (AYP),
    70
America 2000, 65
American Association of Community
    Colleges, 48
American Educational Research
    Association (AERA), ix
Ampere, A. M., 13
Ashby, Ross, 15
Association of Christian School
    International, 68

Bak, P., 19
Barth, M., 71
Bell, T. H., 63
bell schedule, 31, 45, 81, 117
Bertalanffy, Ludwig von, 15
Bestor, Arthur, 54–55, 57;
    Educational Wastelands, 55
Bible, 35
Bilingual Education Act (1968), 62,
    87, 88–89
Bill of Rights, 25–26
Binet, Alfred, 45

biology, viii–ix
Birnbaum, R., ix
Boston Latin School, 26
Brimley, V., 63
Brint, S., 75
Brown, Linda, 56
Brown II decision, 56
Brown v. Board of Education (1954),
    55–56, 85
Buchanan, James, 38
Bullough, R., 52
Bush, George H. W., 65
Bush, George W., 46, 69
butterfly effect, 18. *See also* sensitive
    dependency; tipping point

*Cardinal Principles of Secondary
    Education* (NEA), 42, 85
Carnegie, Andrew, 43
Carnegie Foundation for the
    Advancement of Teaching, 47
Carnegie unit, 46, 83, 117
Carroll, Lewis, *Alice in Wonderland*,
    103
Catholic schools, 34–36, 50, 80–81

change: in complex systems, 8–10; function of, 101; leadership and, 100–106

chaos, complex systems lapsing into, 20, 72, 94, 118–19

Chaos and Complexity Theory Special Interest Group, of American Educational Research Association, ix

charter schools, 65, 67

choice, as educational value, 65–69, 76–78, 92–94, 117. *See also* liberty

Civil Rights Act (1964), 62

classical education, 32–33

classroom management, 9, 10f

Clinton, Bill, 65

Cognitive Edge, x

Cohen, D. K., 31

College Follow-up Study, 52

colleges: in nineteenth century, 37; pre-independence, 26t

Commission on the Relation of School and College of the Progressive Education Association, 52

Committee of Ten, National Education Association, 39–40, 46–47, 82–83

common factors, 103–5

common school movement, 37, 66

community colleges, 47–49, 83

Complexity Society, x

complexity theory: applications of, ix–x; disciplines contributing to, viii–ix; emergence of, vii–viii; fundamental concepts of, 1–22; journals devoted to, x; leaders' use of, 1, 97–123; nonlinear character of, viii, 2–4; organizations dedicated to, ix; technology as aid to, viii. *See also* complex systems

complex systems: causality in, 2–5; cybernetics and, 13–14; emergence in, 14–17; fractals in, 12–13; homeostasis and change in, 8–10; initial conditions of, 17–18; interdependence in, 5; leadership of, 97–123; levels of, 5–6, 6f, 11; nonlinear character of, 119; and reframing, 119–22; rules underlying, 6, 12, 99; sailing metaphor for, 98; self-organized criticality in, 18–20; sensitive dependence in, 17–18; simple, 7–8, 7f; stability of, viii, 3, 18, 21, 72, 74, 76, 88, 113 (*see also* homeostasis); strange attractors in, 10–11; temperamental character of, 18–19, 72, 88, 100, 114. *See also* complexity theory

Complicity (journal), x

compulsory education, 27–28, 36–37, 50–51

Compulsory Education Law (Oregon, 1922), 50–51

Constitution, 25–26, 90, 114

Coolidge, Calvin, 45

Cousin, M. V., *Report on the State of Public Instruction in Prussia*, 66

Cuban, L., 88

curriculum: dumbing down of, 54–55; life-adjustment, 53–55; NCLB's effect on, 70; progressivism and, 44–45, 51–53; and religion, 33–36; secondary school, 39–42, 46–47; standardization of, 45–47, 53; student-centered, 44, 83; and technology, 32–33

Cusick, P. A., 90, 91

cybernetics: in complex systems,
13–14; defined, 13; in family, 14;
leadership and, 111–13; origin of
term, 13. *See also* feedback

Day, C., 105
Declaration of Independence, 25, 90
democracy, 9, 10f
Dewey, John, 44–45, 83
dodo bird effect, 103, 105
Duncan, B. L., 103
dynamic attractors and repellers, 10.
See also strange attractors

Ecclesiastes, book of, 73
Economic Opportunity Act (1964),
62, 63
educational pendulum, 11
educational policy: in complex
system, 72–95; future, 92–94;
interest groups and, 91, 93;
patterns in, 79–82f, 84f, 86–87f,
89f; pendulum of, 75–95; values
underlying, 80–88
educational system: and chaos, 72,
94, 118–19; common factor in,
104–5; complexity of, 23–24, 71;
emergence in, 17; enrollments in,
31, 33, 39, 46, 47, 50, 53, 54, 62,
63; feedback in, 90–91; financial
pressures on, 71, 88; government
role in, 27–29, 36, 41–42, 56–61;
history of, 23–72; homeostasis
of, 76, 91–92; importance of, 74;
initial conditions of, 81, 92; savior
complex of, 75; socialization in,
23–24, 66; strange attractors in, 11;
technology role in, 32–33, 71–72,
88
educational values. *See* values

Education for All Handicapped
Children Act (1975), 61–62, 88, 89
efficiency, as educational value, 31,
44–46, 69, 70, 76–78, 81
egg-crate school design, 31, 44–45,
81, 90, 117
Eight-Year Study, 51–53
80/20 rule, 103–6
Elementary and Secondary Education
Act (ESEA, 1965), 58–61, 63, 65,
87, 88, 92
Eliot, Charles, 40
Elliott, E., ix
emergence: in complex systems,
14–17; of corruption, 16–17;
of habits/routines, 16–17;
leadership and, 113–16; in neural
development, 17; of norms/
assumptions, 15–16
*Emergence: Complexity and
Organization (E:CO)* [journal], x
enrollments, 31, 33, 39, 46, 47, 50,
53, 54, 62, 63
enthusiasm, 105
equality, as educational value, 25–26,
29, 36–38, 49–50, 55–57, 59,
61–63, 69, 70, 76–78, 85
equilibrium: in complex systems, 8–10;
in educational system, 76, 91–92;
leadership and, 100–106. *See also*
complex systems: stability of
ESEA. *See* Elementary and Secondary
Education Act
excellence, as educational value,
25–29, 32, 38, 40, 63–64, 69, 70,
76–78

factory model, 30–31, 44–45
family, feedback in, 14
Farrar, E., 31

feedback: leadership and, 111–13; systems growing in direction of, 14, 18, 112; useful vs. useless, 13, 111–12. *See also* cybernetics
Fields, R., 48
Fisch, R., 120
Ford, Henry, 43
Fourteenth Amendment, 55–56
fractals: in complex systems, 12–13; leadership and, 110–11
Franz Ferdinand, Archduke, 19
Free Schools, 34
Free School Society, 35–36
Friedman, Milton, 66, 90
Fullan, Michael, 1

Gaither, M., 68
Gardner, John, 97
Garfield, R. R., 63
G.I. Bill, 49–50, 85
Gladwell, M., *The Tipping Point*, 18, 117–18
Gleick, J., 10–11; *Chaos*, ix
Goals 2000: Educate America Act (1994), 65, 88, 89
Goldstein, J., vii–viii
government role in education: and accountability, 65; and desegregation, 56–57; in early America, 27–29; importance of, 56–57, 59, 74; local vs. federal, 59–61, 114; *in loco parentis*, 41–42; national security as prompt to, 57–59; parents' rights and, 28, 50–51, 65–66, 68; religious wars and, 36; Smith-Hughes Act and, 41, 114; Sputnik and, 57, 65, 86, 89. *See also* Elementary and Secondary Education Act; No Child Left Behind Act

habits, emergence of, 16–17
Harper, William Rainey, 48
Harris, William T., 40
Hawking, Stephen, vii
Head Start program, 62, 63
Heylighen, F., 14–15
Higher Education Act (1965), 62, 63
high-stakes testing, 70, 102–3
Hill, D. M., 71
history: as complex system, 24; repetition of, 24, 73, 110
history of American educational system, 23–72
homeostasis: in complex systems, 8–10; in educational system, 76, 91–92; leadership and, 100–106. *See also* complex systems: stability of
homeschooling, 68
Hubble, M. A., 103
Hughes, John, 35

Individuals with Disabilities Education Act (IDEA, 1997), 61–62
Industrial Revolution, 30, 42–43
initial conditions, 17–18, 81, 92, 116–18
in loco parentis, 14, 36, 41–42
Institute for the Study of Coherence and Emergence, x
intellectual development, as purpose of education, 42, 55, 57
intelligence testing, 45–46
interdependence, 5, 102
interest groups, 91, 93

Jischke, M., 38
Johnson, Lyndon B., 58, 59, 74
Joslyn, C., 14–15

judgment, 99–100, 108–9
junior colleges. *See* community
   colleges

Kafer, K., 67
Keeney, B. P., ix
keyboard design, 116
Khrushchev, Nikita, 121–22
Kiel, D. L., ix
Kliebard, H. M., 39, 41, 75–76
Koch, R., 3–4
Kridel, C., 52
Ku Klux Klan, 50–51

Lambert, M., 103
Lancaster, Joseph, 30
Lancaster model, 30
land-grant institutions, 38
Land Ordinance Act (1785), 29
leaders: credibility of, 109;
   organizations mirroring qualities
   of, 12–13, 111;
leadership: and change, 8–11,
   100–106; complexity theory's
   usefulness for, 1; of complex
   systems, 97–123; and cybernetics,
   13–14, 111–13; and emergence,
   14–17, 113–16; and fractals,
   12–13, 110–11; guidelines for,
   99–100; and homeostasis, 8–11,
   100–106; judgment necessary
   for, 99–100, 108–9; methods not
   crucial to, 104–5; process crucial
   for, 109; and reframing, 119–22;
   sailing metaphor for, 98; and
   self-organized criticality, 18–20,
   118–19; and sensitive dependence,
   17–18, 116–18; and strange
   attractors, 11–12, 106–10
Lenin, Vladimir, 23

liberal arts education, 32–33
liberty, as educational value, 25–26,
   28–29, 35, 36, 49–51, 69. *See also*
   choice
Life Adjustment Movement, 53–55
Lincoln, Abraham, 38
linear frame of reference, 2–4
Lips, D., 67
Loney, Kate Deadrich, 59
Lorenz, Edward, viii, 18

Mandelbrot, Benoit, 12
Mandelbrot set, 12
Mann, Horace, 37, 43–44, 66
Marion, R., ix, 3
Marshall, Thurgood, 56
Martin, R., 97
McCabe, J. A., vii, viii
McGuinn, P. J., 59–60, 69–70
military logistics, viii
Miller, S. D., 103
Milwaukee Parental Choice Voucher
   Program, 65
monitorial schools, 30
Morgan, J. P., 43
Morrill, Justin Smith, 37–38
Morrill Act (1862), 37–38, 82
Morrill Act (1890), 38
Morrison, K., ix, 5
Morse, Wayne, 61

National Association for the
   Advancement of Colored People
   (NAACP), 56
National Commission on Excellence
   in Education, 63–65
National Defense Education Act
   (NDEA), 57–59, 86
National Education Association
   (NEA), 41, 89; *Cardinal Principles*

of Secondary Education, 42, 85; Committee of Ten, 39–40, 46–47, 82–83; Committee on the Reorganization of Secondary Schools, 42; *Report of the Committee of Ten on the Secondary School Studies*, 46–47

A Nation at Risk (National Commission on Excellence in Education), 58, 63–65, 89

NCLB. *See* No Child Left Behind Act

NEA. *See* National Education Association

new deal, 43

No Child Left Behind Act (NCLB, 2001), 46, 61, 69–71, 88, 89, 91–92, 94, 101–2, 110

nonnegotiables, 11, 107

nonsectarianism, 34, 36

norms, emergence of, 15–16

Northwest Ordinance (1787), 29

Office of Economic Opportunity, 62

Palmer, P., 105

parents: control of education by, 28, 50–51, 65–66, 68, 94; feedback from schools to, 14; *in loco parentis*, 14, 36, 41–42; responsibility for children's education, 27

Pareto, Vilfredo, 103

Parks, Rosa, 117

Pasteur, Louis, 97

Peck, S., 5

phase space, 10–11

Pierce, Walter, 51

Pierce v. Society of Sisters of the Holy Names of Jesus and Mary (1925), 51, 85, 90

Plato, 13

Plessy v. Ferguson (1896), 55–56

point attractors, 9

policy. *See* educational policy

postsecondary education: in early America, 26–27; G. I. Bill and, 49–50, 85; Land Grant Acts and, 38–39; President's Commission on Higher Education and, 48, 50; *Yale Report* on, 32–33, 80

Powell, A. G., 31

power laws, 20

precedent setting, 115

President's Commission on Higher Education, 48, 50. *See also* Truman Commission Report

Principia Cybernetica (website), 15

private schools, 68

progressivism, 43–45, 51–53, 55

Prosser, Charles, 53

Prosser Resolution, 53, 85

Protestantism, 35–36

Prussia, 66

public schools, 30

Public School Society, 34–35

Reagan, Ronald, 64

reductionism, 2–4

reform. *See* educational policy

reframing, 119–22

Reich, R., 74

religion, and curriculum, 33–36. *See also* Catholic schools

repetition, in complex systems, 24, 73, 110–11

Report of the Committee of Ten on the Secondary School Studies (NEA), 46–47

Rhodes, John, 61

Rickover, Hyman, 54, 57

Riis, Jacob, 43
Rockefeller, J. D., 43
Roosevelt, Franklin D., 43
Roosevelt, Theodore, 43
root causes, 2, 102
Rosenzweig, S., 103
routines, emergence of, 16–17

Sanders, T. I., vii, viii
Santa Fe Institute, ix
Santayana, George, 73
SAT exam, 46
scale, common rules operating
    regardless of, 6, 12
secondary school curriculum, 39–42,
    46–47
segregation, 55–57
self-organized criticality: in complex
    systems, 18–20; leadership and,
    118–19
sensitive dependence: in complex
    systems, 17–18; leadership and,
    116–18. *See also* tipping point
"separate but equal," 55–56
Serviceman Readjustment Act (1944).
    See G.I. Bill
shopping mall model, 31, 42
slippery slope argument, 114–15
Smith, Adam, 66, 69, 80; *The Wealth
    of Nations*, 28
Smith, Howard, 61
Smith-Hughes Act (1917), 41, 83, 114
social capital, 14
socialization, 23–24, 66
social science, viii–ix
Society of Sisters of the Holy Names
    of Jesus and Mary, 50–51
special needs, 62
Sputnik (satellite), 57, 64, 65, 86,
    89

square deal, 43
Stalin, Svetlanka, 121–22
standardized tests, 46. *See also* high-
    stakes testing
standard student credit hours. *See*
    Carnegie unit
Stanford-Binet IQ Test, 45
strange attractors, 7; in educational
    system, 11; explained, 10–11;
    leadership and, 106–10; levels of
    complexity determined by numbers
    of, 11
student-centered learning, 44, 83
Swinton, L., 2
symmetry across scales, 110. *See also*
    fractals
systems approach, ix, 15

Tarbell, Ida, 43
Taylor, Frederick, *Principles of
    Scientific Management*, 45, 83
technology: and complexity theory,
    viii; curricular responses to,
    32–33; educational role of, 71–72,
    88
Terman, Lewis, 45
timing, 118
tipping point, 18, 37, 88, 92, 106, 116,
    117. *See also* sensitive dependence
Title VI, 61, 63
Title VII, 62, 63
Title IX, 62, 63, 88
Truman Commission Report, 85. *See
    also* President's Commission on
    Higher Education
tuition tax credits, 66

Uhl-Bien, M., ix
U.S. Department of Education, ix, 60,
    63, 68, 114

U.S. Department of the Interior, 60,
    114
U.S. Office of Education, 53–54. *See
    also* U.S. Department of Education
U.S. Supreme Court, 108, 109

values: choice, 65–69, 76–78, 92–94,
    117; competing, 78, 89–91,
    107–8; educational reforms by
    predominant, 80–88; efficiency, 31,
    44–46, 69, 70, 76–78, 81; equality,
    25–26, 29, 36–38, 49–50, 55–57,
    59, 61–63, 69, 70, 76–78, 85;
    excellence, 25–29, 32–34, 38, 40,
    63–64, 69, 70, 76–78; industrial,
    31; liberty, 25–26, 28–29, 35,
    36, 49–51, 69; motivating force
    of, 73; as nonnegotiables, 11;
    original American, 25–26, 90,

107–8; system structured by, 79f;
    unintended consequences of, 77–78
Viteritti, J., 67
vocational education, 32–33, 37–38,
    40–41, 48, 53
vouchers, 28, 36, 65–67, 94, 117

War on Poverty, 58, 59, 74
Washington Center for Complexity
    and Public Policy, ix
Watzlawick, P. D., 120
Weakland, J., 120
Wheatley, M., x
Wiener, Norbert, ix, 13
Williams, John, 60
women, equal opportunities for, 63
World War I, 19

Yale Report, 32–33, 80

About the Authors

John R. Shoup currently serves as an associate dean in the School of Education at California Baptist University in Riverside, California. He earned a Ph.D. in education from University of California, Riverside. He earned a master of divinity and a master of arts in counseling psychology from Trinity International University in Deerfield, Illinois. He has authored one book on leadership development, teaches leadership and policy at the graduate level, and has conducted workshops on leadership development and best practices from complexity science.

Susan Clark Studer is professor of education and the research coordinator for the School of Education at California Baptist University. She earned her Ph.D. from the University of California, Riverside. Prior to her position at CBU, she taught in public schools for many years. Her research focuses on the historical foundations of education and teacher motivation. She is the author of *The Teacher's Book of Days: Inspirational Passages for Every Day of the Year*. She teaches graduate-level courses in beginning and advanced research and current issues in education and gives talks to local community organizations and schools.